What's in a Name?

MEMOIR, NON-FICTION, POEMS, FICTION

A Collection by the OLLI

Concord, CA Writing Group

2014

Edited by
Elaine Starkman
Donna Van Sant

dvs Publishing
2824 Winthrop Ave.
San Ramon, CA 94583

Book Layout ©2013 BookDesignTemplates.com
Cover design by Donna Van Sant

What's in a Name? Memoir, Non-fiction, Poems, Fiction   A Collection by the OLLI Concord, CA Writing Group 2014
Edited by Elaine Starkman, Donna Van Sant.
June 2014   1st edition.

Printed in the USA by dvs Publishing

ISBN 978-0-9883006-9-9

To Elaine Starkman
Teacher, Writer, Confidant

The Concord OLLI Writing Group, 2014

Deirdre Allan	*Anindita Basu*	*Johanna Best*
George Buice	*Maya Mitra Das*	*Gretchen Davis*
Karoline DeMartini	*Carol Emerson*	*Alan Gould*
Sandy F Higgins	*Stan Husted*	*Kymberlie Ingalls*
Roy Kahn	*Jane Louise Loebel*	*Jennifer MacDonough*
Dave McCauley	*Wayne H. Neal*	*Rule Rattray*
Sylvia Rosenthal	*Marisa Samuels*	*Christine Tomerson*
	Donna Van Sant	

Introduction

We are proud that we've pulled ourselves together in a short, rushed time to present our newest collection:

What's in a Name?
MEMOIR, NON-FICTION, POEMS, FICTION
A Collection by the OLLI[1] Concord, CA Writing Group 2014

It's quite miraculous that we were able to become *"Allies in Astonishment"* this quarter. There is no question that our work is slowly, constantly improving, that we set aside our impatience and continue to work at our writing.

In our third book at OLLI, East Bay Concord, we've managed to combine four genres of writing this quarter; fiction, non-fiction, memoir and poems.

Without the help of Donna Van Sant and her newly formed *dvs* Publishing enterprise, this book would not exist. Thanks, too, to Roy Kahn for post-production assistance. We continue to learn from one another at various levels and experience, and find that our work lives, not just for ourselves, but for new writers as well.

We thank Dita Basu for inspiring the title of the book.

We lost two of our fine long-time writers, Byron Citron and Sarah Simmons. Both were committed to our classes; Byron published a memoir of his experiences at Iwo Jima in *The LLI Review: Fall 2011 volume 6*, (still available online at the OLLI National Resource Center) and Sarah, a PhD in French, slowly allowed us into her early life in Egypt, through both poems and stories.

Blessings, Elaine Starkman

---

[1] Osher Lifelong Learning Institute, at CSUEB Campus, Concord, CA

Contents

{ 1 } Memoir & Non-Fiction

{ 2 } Poems

{ 3 } Fiction

Memoir
&
Non-Fiction

Pioneer Baby

I'M LYING ON A BED, I think it has a cast iron headstand. My belly feels like it's being shoved through a wringer and I'm counting the praying mantis on the ceiling to take my mind off the pain. A bright green lizard skitters up the wall, and a masked stranger is shouting "push!"

It's 1966. I'm in a hospital in a tiny backward town in Queensland, Australia. It's a hot starry night and I'm having a baby.

My husband, our twenty month old son and I had been living in the Land Down Under for a year. He'd been sent by his San Francisco based company to work on a project there.

I felt like a pioneer in this mysterious land where the kookaburras sang, roadsides warned of kangaroos crossing, the Southern Cross twinkled in the black sky, and the water went down the drain backwards.

A few months after our arrival I found myself sitting across the paper-strewn desk of the only doctor in town. His office was small and dark despite the open louvers on the windows. He was a middle aged man. Dark circles under his eyes betrayed fatigue. The instruments in the dusty glass-front cabinet looked even older and more tired than he did.

"You're having a baby my dear," he said as he pushed his smudged glasses up the bridge of his nose. "I deliver my Mums up at the hospital; I'll give you a nice dose of chloroform and then you'll have ten days to rest in bed.

"Chloroform?" I gasped. "I don't want chloroform!" I didn't want to hurt his feelings by saying that it hadn't been used in the U.S. since before the Second World War.

"Well, you see, it relieves labor pains and I don't like to see my Mums suffer."

So much for my idea of pioneering. Suddenly it had lost all its glamour. Here I was, stranded in *Nowheresville* Australia. I didn't want to leave my husband and small son to have my baby thousands of miles away in a less antiquated facility and by a more up-to-date doctor. What on earth was I going to do?

The answer came in the form of a lively young guy who was sitting beside me at dinner one night. He and his wife had just moved up from Sydney to Gladstone. I asked him why he had come to this isolated little town.

"I'm setting up a medical practice here. I've just finished my internship and want to work in a small community."

"Ah! So you'll be delivering babies?"

"Of course," he answered, as he swallowed the last of his fourth beer, "I've delivered the required twenty five in my obstetrical rotation."

"Do you use chloroform?"

"Good God no! That went out years ago."

Here was my savior. I turned to him and asked "Could my baby be your twenty-sixth?"

Once established with the "new young doctor", as he was called, I received a letter from the hospital. It contained a date for a tour and a list of things to bring upon admission.

The first item threw me for a loop. I was to bring a night gown which I didn't want to keep to wear during delivery as it would be burned afterward. I envisioned a huge smokestack on the hospital roof with smoke curling from it spelling the words "It's a boy!"

Nappies, the list went on, soap, shampoo, towels and wash-cloths for the baby. Kotex, soap, shampoo and towels for me. I expected the next item to be groceries, but it appeared they were going to feed me.

I had to go and check this place out. It sounded medieval or at best somewhere where Florence Nightingale roamed the corridors with her lamp.

The small white-washed one story building, topped with a red tile roof, stood at the top of a hill overlooking the harbor. A small struggling lawn divided the gravel driveway from the front entrance, and wilted hibiscus bushes stood beneath the open windows.

The linoleum floors in the hallways were covered in a fine dust and a strong antiseptic smell mingled with unidentifiable odors from the kitchen. A middle-aged, no-nonsense looking nurse greeted me.

"Doctor said to expect you, so I'm here to give you a tour of our little hospital. Follow me if you will." Obediently I followed her starched veil and apron as she rustled down the hall past the patient rooms. They were small. The walls were in need of paint, as were the chipped enamel bedsteads. Threadbare bedspreads were tucked tightly under the sagging mattresses.

"We don't do things the way the Yanks do," she announced as she opened the swinging doors into the delivery room. "No hard tables and stirrups, just a nice cozy bed to have the baby in." Crossing the dark, airless room she pulled a handle that opened the louvers at the window. Immediately a bright green lizard skittered up and across the wall to peer down at a group of dazed flies hovering over the chipped enamel sink.

"But there's a lizard in here, and there's no screen on the window," I protested.

"Not to worry dear, screens cut the breeze and the lizards eat the flies. Right! Run along now, we'll see you in a few weeks."

Not at all reassured, I went home to choose a nightie I was willing to burn.

The last few months were spent in a haze of tropical heat. My belly swelled, my feet swelled, and I waddled around barefoot, flapping my homemade maternity dresses to create my own air conditioning which otherwise didn't exist.

Relief from this misery was found at a nearby sparkling beach where I spent the last day of this swollen torture rocking weightlessly in the rolling waves. I vaguely worried that a near-by shark may be attracted to the pink ruffle of my swimsuit, but that concern was far outweighed by the bliss of being cool.

Labor began that night. I lay in the hot damp sheets practicing my self-taught natural childbirth breathing as my husband frantically urged me to get to the hospital.

"I'm not going to that insect-infested place until I absolutely have to," I insisted in what I thought was a brave pioneer voice. "See how well this breathing is going!"

Less than an hour later we were speeding through the darkened streets of the sleeping town. Gravel flew as the car screeched to a stop outside the front door of the dreaded hospital. Before I knew it I was flying down the hallway in a high-backed wooden wheelchair and a nurse was shouting, "Don't push! The doctor's not here!"

The delivery room bed stood high and menacing in the dim light. "Up you hop," urged my fearless nurse. "Have you brought your bag? Ah, good, is this the nightie you're going to wear? Right, just pop it on and doctor will be here soon."

All this hopping and popping distracted me from the need to push, and I lay there counting the wildlife on the ceiling and walls. *Breathe in, one praying mantis, three flies, two lizards; breathe out, six praying mantis, four mosquitoes, a spider.* Suddenly the swinging doors banged open and in flew David Douglas, my "obstetrician." He was wearing shorts, a tee shirt advertising Queensland beer, and flip flops. As the nurse guided his flailing arms into a gown he kicked off his sandals, one of which barely missed my head as it flew across the room.

"There's no hot water tonight, doctor, so we'll have make do with cold," he's informed as he started scrubbing his hands.

"Shit!" he cursed. "This place is a wreck!"

My daughter arrived a few minutes later, healthy and howling, "She's fit as a fiddle," the nurse tells me with her first smile of the day.

"We did a great job, right?" David asked.

"Yes, but why on earth did you kick your flip flops off?

"Oh, I get better traction barefoot. OK then, I'm off to join your hubby in a few beers, see you in the morning!" The double doors slammed and he was gone.

"Right now, we'll freshen you up, shall we?" asked my dutiful nurse. There's no hot water, but we'll do what we can," she said, as she scrubbed me with a washcloth that felt like it had been dipped in the Arctic Ocean. "Now, that's better isn't it?"

It wasn't. I was shivering and biting back tears. Next I was told to "hop down" from the bed. I sat up, head spinning, and looked down at the peeling linoleum floor. It seemed miles away, and the thought occurred to me that there might be a snake lurking down there. Screwing up my courage I got down and staggered on my jelly-like legs across the room to the Edwardian wheelchair.

Once I was tucked under the much-mended mosquito net over my hospital bed I realized I was starved and asked for something to eat.

"Kitchen's closed dear, you just nod off now and sleep. You need your rest so you can be a good Mum."

The "good Mum" went to sleep dreaming of hot coffee, scrambled eggs and toast dripping with butter.

I woke up to the sound of clattering dishes and peculiar aromas of food. The mosquito net was pulled back and I was handed a heavy wooden tray which held a teapot and a plate covered with a metal dome. My mouth watered as I lifted it up. I saw rice. I saw a mound of grey, evil smelling lumps on top of the rice.

"Is this breakfast?" I asked in a quivering voice.

"Lovely curried lamb; it'll put meat on your bones."

The dam burst. Tears flowed like a waterfall. I sobbed until I couldn't speak. I howled and moaned with longing for home, for my mother, and for scrambled eggs and buttery toast.

My pioneer spirit flew out the screen-less window.

Anindita Basu

What's In a Name?

"AGAIN, WHAT'S THE NAME YOU'VE SAID?" The woman asks me while she goes through my application.

"Anindita, Anindita Basu."

"Quite phonetic—isn't it? A-N-I-N-D-I-T-A. How melodious. Does it have a meaning?"

"Well, it means... hmm... someone not blamed or criticized... like... hmm, beyond judgment, I think."

"How fascinating. Also a bit exotic."

She takes a few minutes and then starts, "Now, Ms. Basu, what made you apply for this job?"

"Hmmm, I wanted to work at a bank, as I mention in my application. I have an Econ major, and I like this place."

"Okay! So you have a B.A. in Economics. Have you ever worked in a financial institution?"

"No ma'am, I just got out of college, got married and came to the U.S."

"When did you arrive?"

"About five months ago. March 6, 1975."

"I see. So where did you work? Perhaps sales?"

"No, ma'am. Nowhere. This will be my first job experience."

First job experience, hmm. I could see a faint smirk come and go. From the top of her bifocals, (Sue Smith, I saw the name on her nametag and desk) she threw this question at me.

"So tell me, Ms. Basu, why should I hire you? What is your strength?"

"Because you want to give someone new to your country a first chance." *It just burst out of my mouth. I didn't mean to be bossy. What do I do now? The words darted around my head.*

I gulped and very slowly tried to manage—"I am a fast learner. I'm very flexible. I have a highly adapting power, people say."

"Highly adapting power." Sue Smith smiles.

Had I spoken correctly? In my mind I thought –I've learned a lot in these five short months... I quickly got used to the fact that the cars and busses ran at the wrong side of the road in this country and though the dime is half the size compared to the nickel, it has double the monetary value... and... and—but I did not say these words. It would have cost me too much of translating. I simply smiled.

"All right. Now let me inform you a bit about this job. You'll have to handle large amounts of money at the busiest time of the day. We are looking for a lunch floater. You'll have no lunch break and will work when the other tellers will be taking their lunch breaks in turn. Your hours will be from 10 am to 2 pm. And right now you'll have no benefits. The pay is low with your starting, you know, about $4.15 per hour."

She looked at me again from the top of her bifocals, meaning—*what do you think?*

"That's fine," I said. "I love the hours and am covered by my husband's medical benefits."

"Very good. If we decide to hire you, we'll give you a call."

The next morning I got a call asking me if I could come in right away. I received a lot of training on the very first day: how to process a check, how to check the signature cards, how to read a microfiche, how to balance at the end of the day, and most importantly, how to serve a customer professionally.

"Always address a customer by his or her name, if possible. Quickly look at the check if you don't know or remember; the name is very important." Ms. Smith made sure that I understood.

Soon, one day I hear, "I must tell you something about your name. We'll give you a name tag you'll be wearing and a plaque to stand right in front of your window."

I was excited!

"Now dearie, how would you like us to call you, I mean to address you? Ani or Dita?"

I was shocked. Very recently I lost my maiden last name by the virtue of marriage. I never knew it would hurt so badly.

"Ani is fine?" Sue Smith looks at me quizzically.

To myself I think, *No, no. I'm not an Annie or Ani. At least Dita has something exotic about it. Someday I'll get used to it.*

"I'd rather prefer Dita."

"Dita Basu you are."

So this is who I'll become in my new country.

Johanna Best

Contrasts—The Right and the Upright

A WWII Story

"THANK YOU SO MUCH for the phone call—and the story! Talk to you, soon. 'Bye!'"

Annelise! Like an open photo album, pictures crowded my mind, I felt stunned. What a story! It took me back – so long ago.

That morning – in spring, 1942 – I met Jutta in front of my house on the way to school. We were both in the 6th grade. She lived about five minutes away from me, across the *Ewalder Busch*. Sometimes, we walked together.

"Did you hear the awful sound, last night?" she asked.

"Of course, I did. Annelise's Dad said it was a shot-down plane, and it must have crashed not far from here."

"Yes, right across from our house, in the woods. I went with my father to look at it after the siren sounded the all clear. I was so mad at the pilot I kicked him! He was dead, you know."

"You did what?" aghast, I looked at her.

"What's the matter with you, he was trying to kill us! He's our enemy and doesn't deserve better." Jutta looked at me suspiciously, and her thick eyebrows almost met where her nose began.

I drew back, *maybe she's a Nazi*. Mother always cautioned us not to talk about that. Timidly I said, "I'm thinking about my brothers and hope nothing like that will happen to them!"

"It would be an honor to die for the *Vaterland!* (Fatherland)," she said theatrically.

"Do you have a brother in the war?"

"You know, I'm the oldest in the family!"

Yes, I knew; she didn't get the point. But I didn't give up. "And your father?"

"He has an important post at the *Heimatfront* (home front)." I felt her appraising side glance.

We had just arrived at Annelise's door and dropped the subject. Annelise, my best friend, joined us. She looked a bit uneasy; I knew, she didn't like Jutta.

"Did you go back to sleep after the air raid?" I asked.

"No, I did not!" She answered in monosyllables, rather unusual for her. It had been a frightful night in our air-raid shelter.

Annelise lived with her parents in a rustic, half-timbered cottage without a basement. Only a field separated our houses. They were assigned to our shelter. After a second trip to the shelter, we all were fed-up. Then we heard this strange, God-awful sound. It wasn't the whistling tune of an approaching bomb before it hits its target, it was a drone that grew louder, louder, and ended in a big BANG, but no explosion followed. Annelise's Dad said, "It sounds like a hit plane crashed nearby."

While Annelise and I walked quietly, Jutta kept complaining about homework, and not getting enough sleep until we reached the *Heideschule*. Everyone discussed that strange noise during the night, and Jutta excitedly told all that the plane had smashed into the woods across their home. She didn't mention, though, what she had told me.

"After school, Annelise and I hurried to a shortcut across their field. Normally, I tried to avoid the path. The Webers had a goat and Billy goat grazing there, and the latter wasn't very friendly. With Annelise at my side, he behaved. I told her about the conversation I had with Jutta that morning. She listened, but was unusually quiet, even without Jutta being present. Since we saved about five minutes by the shortcut, she came home with me for a moment.

My mother was setting the table. "Do you want to eat with us, Annelise?"

"No, I have to go home," replied my friend. "*Tante* (aunt) Best, what does *'an die Wand stellen'* (to be stood against the wall) mean?"

"You mean to put you in the corner for time out, when you have done something wrong?"

"No, not that. I mean to stand someone up against the wall!" She put some strange emphasis on her words.

"Well, it could also mean to shoot somebody," Mother said hesitantly. "You probably misunderstood something."

"I have to go home, now." Annelise hurried out of the door.

"What were you talking about, this morning?" asked mother.

"With Annelise?" I squinted, thinking. "Oh *ja*, I did tell her about Jutta." I told mother about my conversation this morning.

Mother grew still. After a while, she said. "You're right; it was ugly what Jutta did. Stay friendly when she talks to you, but don't seek her out. Anyway, Annelise is your best friend. Jutta is probably only parroting her parents."

She needn't have warned me. I couldn't forget the picture Jutta had drawn for me. Shortly after this event vacation started, and since the air raids grew more frequent, mother took me to relatives in the Hunsrueck, at the Rhine, where war at the home-front was nonexistent. I even stayed a few months longer after the vacation and went to school there.

Now, after more than 65 years, the past catches up with me and Annelise tells me the rest of the story...

"Do you remember that awful night when that English plane crashed in the *Ewalder Busch*?" Annelise asked on the telephone. Of course I did.

"Well, after we came home from the shelter, the doorbell rang. Dad went to answer it. I followed, though saw nothing more than a pair of long legs in beige pants. Dad told me to go upstairs to my room and get some sleep. The next morning, when I came down for breakfast, I saw my mother carrying a tray with food to the barn.

"For whom is that?" I asked astonished.

"'For the cat, go to eat your breakfast!' Her tone didn't allow any more questions. I obeyed, but I was dying to find out what was going on. Shortly after that you were picking me up for school, remember? Jutta was with you."

"Sure I do, but who was it she was feeding?"

"They didn't tell me yet. Again, I asked what it was all about. They told me the less I knew, the better off I was. I was told, 'anyway, don't breathe anything about this to another person, not even Hanna! If anyone finds out about this, *werden wir an die Wand gestellt*.' (Stood against the wall). That's why I asked your mother what it means, because I didn't know. However, when your mother told me, I was so afraid; you know I lost my first parents. I didn't want to lose my adoptive parents, also. I kept my mouth shut, hard though it was. Nor did I understand why! The next day, my mother dyed some clothes black. Then, after another day, all seemed normal again."

"They never told you what was going on?"

"Not then! Years later, when I was already married, Mother told me. The second pilot of the shot-down plane was able to jump out of it, and the parachute landed in a nearby field. He must have waited until we came back from the shelter. Anyway, he just took his chance, rang the bell, and was lucky. My parents hid him and fed him for a few days, but he wanted to leave, so they decided to dye his suit; Mother said he was smaller than Dad was, otherwise they would have given him some of Dad's clothes to wear. He'd try to get over the border to France. He also promised to write after the war was over. He didn't write the address down but memorized it, in case he was caught; the note could have implicated my parents. He was so grateful, but they never heard from him again."

August 14, 1945

I LOOKED EAST through the shimmer of afternoon heat waves to spot the flat orange front of the bus that would carry me to my doom, hoping to see nothing. But it came anyway, the *N San Francisco*, a fluttering mirage at first, becoming substantial as it neared our stop. Before we boarded, my mother gave me the coin to put in the fare box, and, at ten years old, almost eleven, I felt momentarily proud as I paid. I stepped past the driver, smelling the odor of sweaty bodies, diesel exhaust and cigarettes. Its familiarity comforted me as she pushed me to a seat on the shady side.

Sitting with my nose against the grimy glass, I counted off the districts and streets as we rolled through Oakland; Mills College, Hopkins, Laurel, Dimond, the grind up the hill to the Altenheim, down to Lakeshore, passing the marquee of the Grand Lake Theater, with the enormous sign on its roof; anything to keep my mind off of where we were going and why.

The bus rolled west past Kaiser Hospital, always denounced by my parents as 'socialized medicine,' sped up as we emerged from concrete ramps onto the bay shore, passed the radio towers that always excited my curiosity, and rolled onto the dreary, gray, lightless three lane lower deck of the Bay Bridge. My spirits matched the gloom of that passage, and I was beginning to feel a lump in my stomach.

The reason was plain enough: We were on our way to an oculist in San Francisco, to get my first pair of glasses. I was sunk in despair and my mother was tight-lipped, grim and angry about the whole business. Getting me glasses was an extra expense in a budget that was already stretched to the limit. She'd also had to have a neighbor come in to sit with my five younger brothers and sisters, especially as the youngest, Diane, was only nine months old.

Up to this point, my parents had ignored problems with my eyesight, even though they both wore glasses. I had been falling behind in schoolwork, and told my teacher that I could not see the writing on the blackboard or read numbers on arithmetic papers. Finally, during last semester the school nurse had examined me briefly, and then sent a note home identifying my problem. I guess that made it impossible to delay further. I understood, without being told, that this was all my fault.

We walked out of the Key System terminal to catch a white-faced Market Street Railway streetcar going out Geary. It rolled up, and we stepped up onto the rear platform. My mother handed our fares to the conductor standing there, looking gigantic as I stared up at him, straining the seams of his blue uniform. He tugged the bell-rope twice, and the car jerked into motion as we lurched to seats inside.

The diesel in my nostrils was replaced by the sharp smell of ozone, but I hardly noticed it, wanting to huddle alone with my misery. We had made this trip three weeks earlier to measure my prescription and select frames. So I felt no interest in the route, but instead shut myself off from the sea of people on the streets and the clank and grind of the streetcar, focused on the awful fate that awaited me, the four-eyed pariah I would become. I was only startled out of my sour reverie when another streetcar passed going the other way with a screech and a roar, and rocked our car as it went by.

We got off at Powell Street, at the edge of Union Square. My mother took my reluctant arm and propelled me firmly into the corner building. During the ride up in the elevator, I felt like I was being taken to my execution. After a short wait, while my anxiety mounted, the oculist said she had everything ready, and called us into her examination room. She sat me in the big chair, with its lenses and lights, said some kind words and slipped the glasses, plain round gold-plated steel frames, onto my face, then directed my gaze to the eye-chart on the wall where – yes – I could read the fourth line down. She removed the glasses, took pliers and bent the bows to fit my ears, then settled them on my head. The nose pads squeezed my face, and the bows dug in painfully behind my ears. There was no doubt that the glasses were firmly in place. She said that all was well, and ushered us out of her office.

But all was *not* well! My fears of ostracism were drowned in the horrible fun house I found myself in. When I turned my head one way, the whole world revolved the other way! I looked down at my feet, and the floor was at the level of my knees! Once outside, I looked up and saw that every vertical object, like the lamp posts, had a bright blue line down its left side and a red line down its right.

I felt like I was going to throw up, and stumbled about until my mother grabbed my arm again tightly and marched us down Powell to Market. I could barely keep my feet under me in this altered world.

We took the first streetcar heading down Market, and got off at First Street to walk the long block to the Key System. There were people everywhere, soldiers and sailors in uniform, crowds of civilians on their way home from work. As we walked up the streetcar ramp at the terminal, I heard a low growling wail begin from some distance away that rose ever higher in pitch. I knew instantly that it was the big siren at the Ferry Building, and I could feel the hairs rising on the back of my neck as excitement gripped me. I had known for several days that the siren would signal the end of the war, but I had never dreamed that I would be there to hear it. And here it was!

We paused at the top of the ramp to watch the pandemonium that broke out as people in the plaza below heard that rising wail. I watched through those damnable glasses as people started cheering, some started running. Many were embracing, and uniformed men were kissing girls. A roar went up, almost drowning out the siren's ongoing scream.

But I was not celebrating. I'd been waiting for this ever since our paper had announced the imminent end of the war, and here I was with an enormous headache, half-blind, and ready to vomit. "Can I take them off for a while?" I pleaded. "No, you can't," she barked. "You just keep them on. You'll be wearing them from now on, so, *no*! Now, come on!" She jerked me away from the railing and led me inside.

On the ride home, I couldn't bear the kaleidoscope of blurry images outside the bus, so kept my eyes on the back of the seat in front of me the whole way. My memory of that day fades out with the 'N' carrying us east, its passengers chattering excitedly in contrast to our heavy silence, as it rolls through the paper-strewn streets.

George S. Buice

Max's Rat

I WAS AWAKENED BY A COMMOTION at the foot of our bed, a hopping and pawing by our half-Siamese cat, Max. Usually, Max came in and out during the night through the door to our balcony, which we left open, but tonight's movements were not his usual business.

I sat up quietly in bed, and saw in the dim light from outside that Max had brought in a large, live, Norwegian roof rat and was playing with it on our bed. I stood up, careful not to waken my wife, knowing full well what would ensue if she witnessed the sight.

As I approached the foot of the bed, the rat, with Max right behind him, leaped off and made a beeline for the door which led to our bathroom and walk-in closet. I tiptoed through the door too, closed it to insure that the rat could not re-enter the bedroom, then turned on the lights.

I heard noises from within the closet, found Max rooting around in the clutter of shoes under the dresses. I stepped in gingerly, suddenly aware of my bare feet, not to mention the bare rest of me. I saw a ripple in the fabric of one of the dresses, and a moment later I was face-to-face with the rat, now perched on the top of the row of hangers.

I reached down and grabbed Max, held him up to face the rat, which scuttled back to the floor. I put Max down and started kicking at the shoes, at which the rat raced past me and into the bathroom.

I stepped into the bathroom and closed its door, leaving Max outside. The rat ran behind the toilet, and I flushed him out by snapping a towel at him. He was obviously tiring now, and ran to the door, trying to wedge himself under it, without success.

Inspired, I upended the small wastebasket next to the sink, dumped its contents next to the tub, dropped it over the rat. Then I spread a hand towel on the floor, smoothed it out, and slid the wastebasket slowly onto it. When it was centered, I flipped up the towel ends and, holding them tight in tension, turned the wastebasket right side up. Then I turned out the lights, opened the doors and carried the wastebasket quietly across the bedroom, shaking it to keep the rat from gaining its feet, and took it out onto the balcony, with Max right behind me. With one last shake, I dropped the towel, and launched the rat into the bushes below.

Max was off like a shot to the end of the balcony where he could jump to the ground. I walked back inside, closed the balcony door, put the wastebasket back, and climbed into bed.

"What was that?" my wife asked drowsily. "Oh, just something with Max," I replied. "I'll tell you about it in the morning."

Hell In the Literal Sense

"DADDY, WHERE ARE WE GOING," I chirped, trying my five year old best to keep up with his much longer stride.

"We're going to hell and back, Kiddo," he laughed, as he swung me up in the air holding both my hands. "And here we are at the mouth of hell!! Come on now, down you go." We proceeded slowly down the escalator of the BMT Subway Line; holding tightly onto Daddy and the warm greasy railing as we descended into a dark, sultry cavern, teaming with smelly people. Daddy paid for a token and I was allowed, with the station attendant's blessing, to crawl under the turnstile for free. We immediately stepped onto another escalator which carried us even further down into a dimly lit platform, with even more fetid air.

"Ow, Daddy, I can hardly breathe', I complained, dwarfed by all the large bodies around me.

"Hold on tight, the train's almost here." A screech of brakes and a rush of cold air, and the subway plunged from the shadowy tunnel into the station. Doors slammed open. Daddy lifted me up and we pushed through the crowd, getting seated just as the doors slammed shut again.

"I gotta sit by the window," I pleaded.

"But, there's nothing to see."

"Oh yes there is," I countered, trading my scratchy plastic wicker seat for his. I pressed my nose against the filthy window, cupping my hands around the sides of my face to block out the train car's light. I wanted to see them so badly and this was my chance. Excited and bit terrified, I strained to see the sides of the murky tunnel and tracks beneath. *"It has to be here! Father Michael said it was,"* I pouted to myself.

"Hey Kiddo, we're goin' under the East River now." Daddy looked up from his detective story to see how I was doing. But I was totally focused on trying to conjure up the flames of hell and the pitch fork carrying devils that Father Michael had promised.

"Maybe," I thought, *"they're like fairies—they don't want us to see them. Maybe they're shy. Maybe they sleep in the daytime; maybe they only come out on Halloween. Maybe Father Michael lied,"* I mumbled to myself. Numbed with disappointment, I pulled my face back away from the window.

"Time to get off, it's Wall Street," Daddy interrupted my dampened spirits. "Why the long face?"

"Oh Daddy," I fretted, on the edge of tears. "You promised; you said we were going to hell and back. And Father Michael too. He said in Sunday school that hell was beneath earth and that the devils were dancing below us, waiting to pull us down into sin." Daddy didn't answer right away. We again ascended up out of the gloom through a series of escalators and stairs. As we walked through the old partly-cobbled streets of lower Manhattan to his office on Liberty Street, he finally spoke his mind.

"I'm sorry Kiddo," he said, wrapping me in a warm hug. "We grown-ups say a lot of things we shouldn't, and you kids believe us because you trust us. You're not goin' to see devils in the subway tunnels or anywhere else, and you can tell damn Father Michael I said so."

"But what about angels, are they fake too?" I cried.

"Well now, angels, they're a different story," countered my Dad. And, for the moment, I was mollified.

Karoline DeMartini

Quota Girl

T HE SUN BOUNCED OFF THE STEEL RAILS as our train round-
ed a curve in concert with the mighty Hudson's turning. I,
a bit over dressed for comfort, smoothed the pleats of my new
Pendleton skirt and checked my compact to make sure that my
carefully applied makeup was not too bold.

"Don't fuss so much—you look perfect," snapped my mother.
"Just remember, don't slouch. Vassar girls don't slouch!!"

Shortly, we pulled into Poughkeepsie station and hailed a
taxi for the brief trip to campus. Massive blocks of granite
framed an ivy covered arch which shielded us as we entered the
Vassar grounds. It was all I could have hoped for: a venerable,
safe, secure fortress in which to become socially and intellectu-
ally brilliant. I had always wanted to go to one of the Seven Sis-
ters schools and my mother, self-created intellectual snob that
she was, encouraged my ambitions. Neither of us had a clue
about the lens through which I would shortly be evaluated.

We made our way to the Administration Building, another
granite hulk, camouflaged, softened even, by a dense ivy cloak.
Here, after a brief wait, Mom and I parted ways. I was led
through an oak paneled tunnel, lit with ancient sconces, into a
sun filled circular room anchored by a hummingbird of a wom-
an, all a flutter with papers and files and the accoutrements of
an overworked schedule.

"Come in, Miss De Martini," she beamed. "I hope you and
your mother had a lovely trip up here. Spring always shows Vas-
sar at its very best." I, mindful of my mother's admonitions, low-
ered myself gracefully into the comfortable wing chair offered,

and thus, my genteel interrogator and I began our measured dance of discovery.

I had been well coached. My job was to beam out the image of the perfect "Vassar girl," armed with my outstanding academic record, a trunk full of awards and creative achievements. Hers was to pierce my delicately woven armor. We jousted well together and as the interview wound down, I knew I had held my own.

As we began to disengage and I rose to shake her hand in farewell, my bird woman adversary launched the final weapon in her arsenal. "Oh, Miss De Martini, there's one more bit of information that you should know about us before you leave."

"Oh yes," said I, already basking in what I assumed to be acceptance. She sighed apologetically and delivered her shot.

"We have a quota system for girls like you, and unfortunately, you have two strikes to overcome in our selection process. You're Catholic and also of southern European descent."

"You mean Italian," I sputtered. "But I'm only one eighth Italian," I yelped, my facade of gentility peeling fast.

"I know it must sound harsh," she said, "but our founders established Vassar to educate the daughters of this country's leaders, the established families of our society—I think you understand what I'm saying. Since you're obviously Vassar material, you'll be placed on a special list for consideration, should we have an opening."

"Thank you," I murmured, and beat a retreat back through the oak paneled tunnel to my mom in reception.

"What's the matter?" she hissed, as we exited the building. Holding back tears of frustration, I parried, "Everything's okay--I'll tell you about it on the train."

And so my dreams of being a Seven Sisters graduate were dashed forever. The letters came two months later. For a minute before I ripped open the envelope, there was a shred of hope. But then, the expected rejection floated up from the brief paragraph wishing me well in future endeavors. Smith College was also a "no." My close friends, Anne and Jane, one Catholic, one not, both got in. I was grateful Mom didn't push me to talk about it. I think she, too, needed to regroup.

Such a tiny incident—a mere drop in the bucket, in terms of human misery, but for me, it changed the way I looked at the world. In that brief sequence of events, my seventeen year old self internalized that the pillars of adult wisdom—"play by the rules—work hard and you'll be a success," were fraudulent, and my newly hatched rebel-self began its life long journey to question everything.

Sandy Fitzgerald Higgins

Placeholder

VARIOUS SOULS CONGREGATE ONE DAY A YEAR to eat dinner at the same location, depending if the family is talking to each other. Most everyone lives in California. Recalling my eighth year, I asked with excitement when everyone would arrive. I loved those parties. My mother's nervous voice would go through the list of characters fast in an attempt for me to understand the mixed crew coming through the door, storming the buffet table, leaving behind turkey carcasses and smashed cranberries on the shag carpet.

Mom coughed and cleared her throat saying, "Hold on; it's going to be a bumpy ride. Here, I'll name the good and not-so-good, kind of like a game of rolling a pair of dice, odd numbers beat the house."

So I sat down and, being eight, I listened to understand who belonged to who when I got the rundown on the fun bunch. No matter what, I was told ***not*** to talk to Uncle Stan because he just got out of serving time in San Quentin, Mom telling me, *you can stare but don't smile. If he says anything to you, run to Dad and point your finger. Dad is there with a bag of tricks to urge him out of the door.* Then, in a rush, she quickly continued: *No, the tricks are not Cracker Jack tricks.* From here she kept up running sentences together until she finished, sounding something like this:

Give a big kiss to your Uncle Morris; he's the Four Star General in the U.S. Army, his office is in the Pentagon. His head is clean-shaven so he looks different from Uncle Stan... Stay away from Kathy. When you aren't looking she'll steal your little checkbook. Oh! That's right, you don't have a checkbook yet. Check your discount card you carry in your wallet that gets you into the movie house. Make sure it's still there when dinner's over. Aunt Ellen with the intelligent words and soft voice, who smells like a lilac, cuddle up in her lap. She might sing a verse from La Mancha. Uncle Ray, don't play cards with him, keep your piggy bank tucked into your sock drawer... never bet you can beat him playing Go Fish. Aunty Dolores, she'll take you to her art studio. You can play with her hair if you ask nicely. Be sure to look at her earrings, they're from the Orient. She's a talent artist. Uncle Jack, just stay away. Don't ask why, just stay away. Octopus hands is his nickname. You call him Uncle Jack, okay? Aunt Lorraine, she's the one with long fingers and loves to play the piano. Her son is the musician, remember? Uncle Pete, you might hear his talk of Prisoners of War World War Two camp. Just sit at his feet, and don't ask questions. Just listen. Uncle Morris and Uncle Pete like to sit together at the dinner table and talk. Between Morris and Pete linger a little, our family likes to call them heroes. Aunt Vera, be careful around her. She might get you wet when she spills her drink or maybe it will be just the ice cubes. In that case, put them back in the glass and walk away. Uncle Avery, he is the nice one, remember? He brought you cookies from his long distance sales job... don't eat too much before dinner. I want you to eat a full meal. Uncle Larry, he might talk your socks off so be careful not to sit too close to him. Your cousin Bridget had a pantyhose incident with him. I'll tell you later about that when you're a little older. Aunty Katie, her kisses always leave lipstick whenever she kisses you on your face so turn your head. Let her kiss your hair. If Aunt Sue shows up, she's the whiner but she does not drink.

Uncle George, no, he was not born in Fairyland. Don't tell him we say that each year when he leaves the table. Aunt Ann, she travels the world and knows many men on land and on sea. Just say a prayer under your breath when you hear her talk up a storm. Uncle Ron, he has shiny shoes, loves to dance, he may ask you to join him, so be ready. Aunt Liza, umm. Poor Liza! Walk past her fast. Uncle Hubert, if he's smoking his cigar, make sure ashes don't drop on the carpet. Aunt Kelly, she's the happy one. Ask her to tell you a joke and you can retell it on the playground. She giggles at everything. Uncle Harry, he's not your real uncle; he's left-overs from Aunt Sally's divorce. No, Aunt Sally never comes anymore, but Uncle Harry still knows our door every holiday, rain or shine, preaching he is not the liar... she is...

Then my mom stopped abruptly, gave a big sigh and ended her longwinded tutelage for a moment. Gasping, she continued: "On second thought, I'll tell you about the *other* 14 aunts and uncles, but first I have to run and hide my jewelry before the doorbell rings. Now go off and play till they all get here."

Romance the Second Time Around

MINUTES BEFORE JILL DIED in the emergency room, she reached for my hand. I continued to hold her hand for an hour after she passed away saying over and over, "I love you." I missed so many moments that are gone forever. I realized too late for Jill the expression of love that is generated by holding hands.

Two years after my wife died, I married Allean, one of her best friends. I didn't consciously decide to be more romantic the second time, it just happened. Allean and I hold hands because I know it demonstrates tenderness, and it keeps her from walking too fast and leaving me behind. Walking together through the neighborhood allows us to listen to each other more intently without the distractions of the house, TV, and the dog. My role is to listen and not solve whatever is bothering her.

"I just want you to listen, can you do that?" she says. One of her favorite places to walk is at shopping malls. To me going shopping with her is the ultimate sacrifice, but I do it in the name of love. Shopping with her gives me the opportunity to boost her self-esteem as she tries on clothes. "You look great in that blue dress, Sweetheart," I tell her with every dress.

Another part of being romantic is listening to music together. Allean thoroughly enjoys listening to songs about love from the 1960's. Being the sensitive husband, I subscribed immediately to the satellite radio after we were married so we could have it in our home and car. When Jill died, I started listening to the words of the songs, especially her favorite, "Cherish" by

The Association. Wow! I had never heard those great lyrics. I make sure to pay attention to those songs and artists which are Allean's favorites.

Flowers are as important as chocolate in a loving marriage. It takes so little time to show a caring heart. I try not to underestimate the message that flowers give about my attentiveness and affection. It has become routine to buy cut flowers at the local discount store; fresh flowers are always present in our home. I make them last for two-three weeks by cutting a little off the stems every day and putting them in fresh water. About a year ago I started taking a couple of the flowers and putting them in a small vase on her dresser so she sees them when she wakes up in the morning.

The flowers are a nice touch, but looking back I regret that I did very little cuddling with Jill. *"Can't it be enough to just hold me?"* she would whimper. I am left to wonder how many intimate moments we missed because of her justified fear that I would take her soft kisses or gentle touches as foreplay, instead of her just wanting to be held close. Besides cuddling more, I massage Allean's feet while we watch TV, which relaxes her. Once we are in bed, if she turns towards me, I know that she wants me to rub her hands for a few minutes. That helps her to forget the problems of the day. It doesn't take long for her to fall asleep.

Allean is considerate of me as well. She has stopped dozens of my migraine headaches by massaging my temples where the throbbing pain begins. I lay my head in her lap on a pillow and after 20 minutes of her continuously rubbing, the pain finally subsides. Another thing I adore about Allean is how she sits with me every night while I watch my favorite TV shows. Of course, she is either reading or sewing, but her being there sends that all important message, "I love being with you."

Maybe because we both lost our spouses we understand how important it is not to take the other for granted. Every day we look for ways to do something for each other. It might be something simple like going out and buying her a bagel for breakfast. She will go downstairs to get a snack for me since she knows I get hungry watching sports on TV. Regardless, I learned that being romantic is simple:

Show my love for her every day.

Kymberlie Ingalls

It's All Wrong But It's All Write

The life of a writer.

I'VE HEARD THE ARGUMENTS for either side: that it is solitary, or it is social. All depends, really, which way you want it to go. But it's a hard life. An artist puts a lot of themselves into creating, then comes the judgment. Like a child seeking approval, we want to think that we've pleased the world. We want to stand on a chair, kick up our heels and curtsy in our Shirley Temple dress and curls, and bask in the applause. And, some little atom inside of us has also convinced us that we have unleashed genius upon the world.

Then come the accolades.

Ask us which we remember more – a hundred compliments... or one criticism.

I find this to be true off the page as well. Having grown up in a fishbowl of gunky water polluted by negativity, it's hard to comprehend when I'm swimming in clear water. When someone smiles and says "I love your sweater!" I immediately think "but my hair looks like crap, right?" It's like, one kind word forward, two insults back.

Every week, I take words that I've poured onto a sheet of paper, then I gingerly carry said papers to one of my many critique groups so that they can sprinkle their salt and piss lemon juice all over the wounds.

Okay, I kid. Sort of. Critiques are a very helpful, and necessary tool for any writer. One of the groups I'm in has the "rule" that we can't respond to any comments unless it's a direct question.

At least one of us fails miserably every single week.

It is a very difficult thing to sit silently while people misinterpret your intent. We're writers, for shit's sake. We do what we do to *express ourselves.* Putting a gag order on us is the same as duct-taping our hands to the desk. We want to defend our words to our death! Then come the times when we do let our audience down. Any artist takes that personally, feels it deep inside like a prostate exam gone wild.

Tonight, one of my fellow writers, after hearing two pieces regarding my recent friendship fallacies, earnestly stated that my "voice" has lately seemed a bit too passive. I, of course, want to shout out "Look at the last three months of my life! Being momentarily passive is what has saved that little shred of sanity I have left hanging from the rafters in my head."

I know she meant well, and it's a genuinely helpful comment. But in my head all I can think is—*I failed my audience*. I have not convinced them of my detachment—rightfully earned as I watch people leaving me in droves. Why might that be? Because while I can write these feelings down in blood-red ink, it is followed by my false persona of smiles and polite conversation. I belie my own words with my actions.

Truth, with a side of hypocrisy, please. No just desserts, thank you.

Kymberlie Ingalls

Remembrance of Hope

"I can't tell you where I'm going, not sure of where I've been, but I must keep travelin' til my road comes to an end. I'm out here on my journey, trying to make the most of it. I'm a puzzle, I must figure out where all my pieces fit."

THERE IS SOMETHING TO BE SAID for the open road on a quiet, starry night as the winds whisper and the radio remembers when.

Right now my husband and I are somewhere on the edge of Nevada and Utah as we embark on a much-needed trip to the homeland of cheese curds and football fanatics. It's Grandma's 90th birthday and it'll be a fair family occasion. Wisconsin is a beautiful change of scenery with its cool lakes and lush green woods.

Many are asking why we elected to drive rather than fly. Roger and I share a love of road trips, so the decision to drive even with the high price tag at the gas pump ruled over the 'convenience' of flight. It's an especially difficult decision as business owners to take the extra time, but watching Roger enjoy himself behind the wheel of our truck tells me it was the right thing to do.

That, and he flat out refused to fly with me. I tend to get a little uptight around planes, and with the tenth anniversary the 9/11 tragedy looming, this wasn't the weekend to be getting into skirmishes with airport security.

Our nation is in a horrible place today with its politics and economy, but we are still free to drive our broke asses across the country and take in every touristy sight along the way. We are free to speak out about the injustices around us, free to spend our money foolishly while complaining about our government doing the very same. We are free to support or rally against our military that has been at war since the nightmare that attacked New York City ten years ago in September.

Yes, it really has been ten years. The Pearl Harbor bombing or Kennedy assassination of my generation ("Where were you when you heard the news?) that would alter our freewheeling ways forever. As with the Japanese and the African American races before them, Middle-Easterners became the new enemy to the American public right here on our own land—their home. Families were ripped apart by death and by enlisting soldiers; flags and yellow ribbons splashed across our nation in a sudden patriotic rainbow.

We all came together as a family that day for those who died, and for those who survived. As all families have their dysfunction, such is the state we are in now. Wishes of peace, and of war, have separated us into battle camps here on our own soil. This mess we're in is destroying us—like being on a speeding train that's going to derail and we have no means to stop it in time. Sometimes I hear the screeching of the wheels on the steel rails in my sleep, mingling with the newscasters telling me that unemployment has risen yet again, and another angry homeowner showed up at a bank with gun in hand.

Everything we have worked for has slowly died or withered away. "Don't let them win!" was the battle cry, because the message of the 9/11 attacks was to hurt us financially, and just like a Texan does, Cowboy George came riding in whooping and hollering, dropping bombs and our money along with them.

As *God Bless the USA* faded on the radio, and the economy began to tank, we have turned on each other again.

Where is that American bond now? Where is the brotherly love that gave others hope on that day when our skies were dark and our streets were torn asunder?

As the white lines blur past us in the night, I'll be reflecting on what was lost that morning at summer's twilight—families, hopes and dreams. I'll take photos of the factories and the farms, the corn fields, the hills, mountains and lakes. We'll celebrate Grandma's birthday, enjoy coming together as a family, be thankful for the plentiful bounty, and try to forget that this was a trip we couldn't afford to take but finding the value in the newly created memories.

Along with those overseas, our fighters here at home deserve the same respect—the responders to the 9/11 tragedy who came from far and wide, from the flatlands and the mountains, the hills and the valleys. They made the trek to New York to volunteer themselves for those in need.

I don't support war, nor do I support our involvement in the affairs of other countries, but our men and women are there whether I agree with the reason or not. They are far from home and deserve my gratitude, including my cousin that I only discovered last night was the victim of a roadside bomb in Afghanistan. With any luck, his two broken legs will bring him home.

These are the things I'll be thinking about as the occasional song reminds me of our hometown heroes, and keeps me searching for the common good that rose to the surface of American humanity on September 11th, 2001.

Yes, there is something to be said for the open road on a quiet, starry night.

"Like a poor wayfaring stranger that they speak about in song, I'm just a weary pilgrim trying to find my own way home."[2]

---

[2] Lyrics: *Travelin' Thru* / Dolly Parton

Sing Together

If I run out of songs to sing to take your mind off everything, just smile, sit a while with the sun on your face and remember the place we met.

"YOU HAVE TO WANT TO LIVE FOR YOURSELF." Why? Why do I *have* to? Where is this rule book, and who is the know-it-all behind it?

If there was only me to live for, I'd have checked out a long time ago. It's others who keep me connected, keep me here. It's not always easy—people disappoint me, invade me, mislead me. But, it shouldn't be easy. "It's supposed to be hard. If it wasn't hard, everyone could do it," said the reel-time baseball legend Jimmy Dugan.

When I was young, communicating was very difficult as most anything I found the courage to say had severe consequences - sadness, anger, violence. I learned by trial and jury that words carried weight, and were to be used carefully. Like an hour gone from the clock, they can't be taken back. I was about five years old when I mustered up the nerve to ask my mom to stop calling me "Kimmy." She was delivering my older brother and I back home to my dad's, which always left me in tears, but I really hated that name. I could see she was trying to hold back something in her throat but wasn't doing very well. "My baby is growing up!" I felt just awful, standing on the curb with stones sinking to the pit of my tummy because I just made Mom cry. It would be twenty-five years later before I could assert myself to insist being called Kymberlie over any shortened version of it.

It was in my early 20s when a bout of depression came on. I was tired of my life. I became catatonic, and stopped talking to anyone about anything. Nobody ever listened anyway, so what was the point? This lasted for several months. I went about my same life, but in complete silence. I had lost my voice, literally. Words would flit about in my head, but none found their way out. I don't remember what brought me back, nor do I know which was worse—having nothing to say, or that nobody noticed.

I've learned to express myself, and rarely sit on the edges quietly anymore.

I am thankful for the internet, and the people it has brought into my life. Some I'd never have met otherwise, some I've been given the opportunity to see layers that aren't afforded outside of Facebook or emails. Our encounters may be brief, but I find that better than nothing at all. When I signed up for FB I did the requisite search of classmates and took a chance with reaching out to a few. You see, I'm much more socially courageous than twenty plus years ago. Jim is a boy from my high school, now all grown up. He surprised me one day by remarking on a post of mine with a very encouraging speech that bolstered my spirits, despite that we barely know each other. Turns out he'd been paying attention to all of my status updates and I suspect might have read an essay or two of mine.

We hadn't ever socialized in school; he said this was a valuable lesson he could teach his son. "Get outside of your group as there are awesome people everywhere and it's only artificial constructs that keep us from experiencing real friendships." Something worth learning, but as with everything, the timing matters. Had we looked past the cliques back then, we wouldn't have lived the lives we have. Only takes one step to the side to change an entire existence. The moral of this story is that I like forging these friendships when there is more to bring to the table.

Regardless of the whens and wheres, and despite all the clichés about climbing mountains and the journeys of life, the message is a strong one. Life *is* a journey, albeit a crooked, cragged path. I have to be reminded to look beyond my lonely shadow to see the trees around me. Those trees are the friends who have grown along the way. Without them to raise my eyes from the ground, I would miss the chance to find my words in the cotton candied clouds.

Not everyone wants to live to a ripe old age. I'm not strong enough to keep my feet planted on this side of the grass. My people are why I stay, even when they don't stay for very long. They are chapters, not stories, and I am the teller of their tales. They give courage to my voice.

Without you, I never would be me. You are the leaves of my family tree.[3]

---

[3] Lyrics: *Sing Together* / Train

Roy Kahn

Acapulco—Death and Survival, 1940

FOUR DAYS BEFORE MY MOTHER, my older brother, Ephie and I (aged 14) arrived in Taxco on my mother's search for her deserting lover, the first-ever auto-worthy road to Acapulco opened. Before that, only travel by foot, burro or boat was possible. It, like the road to Mexico City from Texas, was a non-lined, two-lane wide tar-surfaced affair. My mother had decided that we would drive there despite all my objections. *(Hey! The hunt is all!)* We drove there.

In1940 Acapulco was not any kind of a town. When we got there, the office of the hotel at which we had reservations proved to be on a small, flat plot of land set slightly above a cliff-side overlooking a chasm of pounding sea-water two hundred feet below. It was way above invisible Acapulco. The hotel office was a beige one-story adobe cube containing a kitchen, a dining room, male and female toilets, and the 'office'. It was an 'office' because it had a phone. The hotel's 'guest rooms' were completely separate from the hotel. They consisted of four separate caves, carved into a precipitous cliff located a distance below the adobe building. The caves themselves could only be reached via a single, narrow dirt path which ran in front of them. The path was narrow, and on the side away from the caves it dropped a terrifying distance to the sea below. No hand rail. Each cave boasted three hammocks and an unadorned 25-watt electric bulb hanging inside. There were no doors, no toilets; just a sheet to tack up over the entryway at night—for modesty's sake. Toilet and food had to be accessed, day or night, by risking the frightening, unlit pathway in front of the caves, and then climbing up the hill to the house. We were the hotel's only occupants.

From our cave we could see the nightly flights of Mexican boys and men as they sailed off the 200+ foot-high cliffs across the way—throwing themselves to the sea for the handful of viewers down below and for the few centavos tossed at them after each soaring, magical, dangerous dive. They always made it.

I never got into the port-town of Acapulco, so I cannot describe it. But somehow—*God knows how!*—my mother got herself into town and actually succeeded in locating her New-York-City-riding-master-ex-lover there and, apparently, 'had it out' with him. She was mightily pleased with herself. She even found time to smile and pat me on the head occasionally.

Freed from her fury of pursuit, she wound up meeting new people – all tourists – one of whom was one-half of an allegedly-married couple. Each partner had a different last name, which was simply unheard of in 1940, but no one disputed their alleged legitimacy. They said they were from England. The woman said that her name was 'Marguerite Long', and both claimed that she was 'a concert pianist'. Her 'husband' was, in my 14-year-old's judgment, an Irish 'Nothing'. A man named Armand Conn was travelling with them, and my mother 'took up' with him. He was single, decent-looking and claimed to be a high school teacher in New York City. He wound up doing the driving for us instead of my brother Ephie, which pissed off Ephie no end.

About 30 minutes after we drove away, going toward Taxco, on Mexico's brand new road, we saw a gaggle of 'peasants' peering from the edge of the road into a gully. Curious, we stopped. A car had apparently gone off the road and careened down the green hillside. The car was about 100-feet down. After taking this in, we discovered that two men, who turned out to be Americans, had been rescued and were lying on the ground just off the road. One had a pulsing, bleeding gash in his forehead and had lost his voice; the other had a compound-fracture of his right arm and cuts all over his face. The one who had the head injury and had lost his voice was a pianist, and the one with the broken arm turned out to be a singer. It was dumb luck for each of them that the injuries were not the other way around.

Despite the fact that we had not seen a single vehicle on the new road for our entire Acapulco trip so far, a truck miraculously appeared and the Mexicans loaded the singer onto its flatbed. The truck took off down the highway towards Taxco. We gentled the pianist, voiceless and bleeding, into the back seat of our car, and drove off, also towards Taxco.

Armand was behind the wheel, and was driving pretty fast. We wanted to get our injured American to a doctor as soon as possible. The road abutted an on-going ditch that ran along the steep-rising hills on the left side of the road. The other side of the road descended equally steeply. About thirty minutes en route, a peasant leading a burro suddenly appeared from nowhere. He had been hidden in the hills by the wild bushes to our left, and just stepped out of them directly into the path of our car. Despite Armand's swerving efforts to avoid him, the man was hit and thrown forward for a good forty feet. I saw that his face was ripped off; then he just lay there. Our car careened before stopping in the water-ditch on the uphill side of the road.

From a previously totally deserted landscape, and from all directions, about 2-dozen angry Mexicans with machetes and sombrero-type hats materialized. (These were the days when the Mexican government had to have armed *'Federales'* patrolling all the tourist-used roads in Mexico because these roads were hunting grounds for happy kidnappers and banditos.) We were scared. Armand kept saying *'muy infortunado'* to the peasants as he passed out American cigarettes to them.

The Mexican police arrived from an unseen town and, of course, they arrested us. Not surprising, especially after they looked in the back of our car and found our voiceless, semi-conscious, quietly bleeding prior guest. To them, it must have looked like the *Americanos* were bombing around Mexico, hitting people with their car and then loading them into it and carting them off, for unknown reasons. They took away our still-mute passenger. We were told later that they had gotten him onto the bed of a truck that was headed for Taxco. They also removed the Mexican we had hit – taking him to the local town, where he was found to be already dead.

We were jailed, of course; separately (thank God!) from the Mexican inmates of that overcrowded, filthy, fly-infested, two-room jail, whose single, long-waterless toilet bowl had long ago overflowed with ancient and current deposits and now remained, stinking and fly-feeding, awaiting yet more contributions.

My mother was allowed to telephone the American consulate in Mexico City. I watched her as she made the call from a phone booth. She entered in total calm; once connected, she threw a yelling, tearful 'fit'. The call finished, the 'fit' disappeared. She walked out completely calm again, and said, with assurance: "they will get us out".

That night, we were allowed to stay in an available, empty local house. We were its only occupants. It had running water and electricity. The police sequestered our car as 'evidence'—we knew not where.

I guess that calls were made from Mexico City, because the next day we were brought before a judge. He said that our unfortunate victim was "from the hinterlands" and "probably knew nothing of automobiles and had not seen one before" and "probably thought that a car could rear on hind legs like a horse." We were fined $20.00 U.S. "for the widow" (and the going cost of a life in Mexico in 1940) and we left.

We never again heard of or from the pianist we had rescued (he electing to stay mute in Taxco), nor of, or from, his singer friend with the broken arm.

Neither of them waved goodbye.

David McCauley

Eagle

I FLAPPED MY ARMS, slowly at first but then with more vigor. Rising from the sidewalk in front of our house in Daly City, I worried about the tangle of telephone and power lines that filled the air above me. Zigging and zagging, I finally rose above them and caught a breeze, lifting my six-year-old body into the sky.

With a few more downward pushes, I flew over the *ticky-tacky* houses below as the San Bruno Mountain loomed ahead of me. A familiar updraft lifted me above the green grass-covered hills. I gazed down at the San Francisco Bay ahead. The big city spread out for miles to my left and right. Exhilarated by the total freedom of soaring high above the cares of people below, I swooped around for a while and then began slowly descending toward home. My flying dreams ended here, before the difficulties of landing. They recurred many times in Daly City and Millbrae as I grew into my teens.

Forty years later I learned about the transformative power of our personal totems, the enduring animal symbols that allow people to explore the mysteries of life and the spirit world. Each animal embodies certain strengths and attributes that the spiritual seeker can embrace and follow on the path of self-exploration. After considering the wolf, turtle, and hawk, I chose the eagle as my personal totem, perhaps because of my vivid childhood dreams.

> The eagle is endowed with strength to soar the highest of the birds. If the eagle has revealed itself as your totem animal, you may expect to receive renewed strength of body, mind,

and spirit. You will find your meditations becoming more profound and your visions more prophetic. If you maintain a harmonious and balanced lifestyle, you will feel a stronger connection to the Great Mystery than ever before in your spiritual pilgrimage on earth. [4]

I felt a connection to Chief Dan George and enjoyed his movie appearances. While traveling in his native land of British Columbia, I spied his small book, *My Spirit Soars*. It tells of the wisdom of this eighty-year-old Native American as death approached him in 1981. He speaks about nature and his people. The epilogue ends with, "When Chief Dan George was buried, his family and friends watched in awe as an eagle appeared overhead and flew, in silent circles. After the ground had swallowed his casket, the eagle disappeared into the clouds."

---

[4] TOTEMS, Brad Steiger, 1996.

David McCauley

Pre-Teen Encounter

"ON YOUR MARK, GET SET, GO!" Our "inside" feet were tied together at our ankles with a small piece of rope. My partner in the three-legged race was a girl about my age of ten, whom I had never seen before. I'd never been this close to a girl, our legs touching from ankle to thigh. She happened to be standing near me in the pre-teen area of the kid's games at the 4th of July Picnic. It was 1953 at the Capuchino High School baseball field in Millbrae.

We took off across the field but soon tripped and fell with our arms and legs flying in all directions. Up we stood and were off again in a second dash toward the fifty-yard turnaround point. As we turned to go back I whispered, "Put your arm on my shoulder like they're doing," looking toward the two kids about ten yards in front of us.

"Let's slow down and get in step," she responded. In a half-embrace now, I felt awkward from the touching, but connected as we moved in unison.

We moved steadily past three other teams with no more falls and only two pairs arriving at the finish line before us. I quickly untied the rope and stepped back from her, as we turned our attention to the others crossing the finish line.

A few minutes later we said "Bye", as we smiled at each other and our white, third-place ribbons, never to cross paths again.

Wayne H. Neal

The Dance Lesson

MY MOST EXPENSIVE DANCE LESSON, ever, was free. It carried a value I would never see the rest of my life. I got it through strategic planning, much like military generals plan battles. My tactics yielded the latest state-of-the-art methods. Coaching from my instructress drove me to show off my most accomplished steps.

In 1942, as a young man of six years, my plans were perfect. I knew they would work because I patterned them on the success of the most talented individual available. But they say everything has its price; had I known the *real* cost awaiting me, I might have studied another subject.

Success revolved around the actions I planned for the kitchen. The moment I opened the door I visualized the outcome of my historic scheme. My mother ruled the kitchen with authority, not that I thought she lacked it elsewhere, but I had a mission to accomplish and like any good general, I would do my duty.

She worked steadily at the wood burning cook stove, a necessity, because few homes in rural America at the time, had gas, electrical power, or running water. A fast-paced tune entitled "Ida Red" came out of the battery radio.

The cook stove, an ingenious device, had a hot water reservoir, an oven, and a cooking surface. A bread warmer perched high above the cooking surface. Thus equipped, my mother gave tested definition to the term "multi-tasking" sixty years before computers.

Special tools rested atop the bread warmer. In particular, it cached a unique contrivance, the most imposing device of all, and arguably the most useful. It became the center point of my dance career. The tool continuously occupied the flat surface atop the bread warmer, that is to say continuously, except when in use. It was an awesome implement my mother called a switch. Not a switch in the ordinary sense of the word, however. One perhaps visualizes a light switch, but this particular switch lit-up people, not light bulbs. The best way I can describe it is to compare it to a magic wand. She used it to work miracles. Among the seven siblings, I knew I was a favored son because she performed its magic on me most often; it regularly inspired me to improve myself.

Character determined its worth. My mother, an excellent judge of character, demanded a perfect switch. I learned from her that good character is better than bad character. Anytime *my* character displeased her she would command, "Young man, you go to the orchard and cut me a right keen switch from a peach tree."

Invariably, my first character analysis did not meet her standards.

"Young man, that switch is not good enough; it's too small. You get right back out there and cut a bigger one!" An astute no-nonsense person, she accepted no substitute for quality.

Although 1942 was a time of severe rationing because of World War II, we never lacked nutritious meals prepared from the products of farm harvests. Other items were simply unavailable, in short supply, or almost impossible to obtain. The military exercised first choice of even the most basic items, such as sugar, coffee, flour, and gasoline. My family, for example, considered peanut butter, crackers, and store bought candy a luxury. Those items rarely found their way to our house. When they did, it was on special occasions like Christmas or Independence Day. We relished those events and envied the more privileged who could buy them frequently.

*   *   *

One fortunate family lived nearby. Luckily, for me, the family had a son about my age. We played cowboys and Indians when we got the chance, much to the chagrin of my mother. I say chagrin because fortune has a way of creating social classes. Social classes create social distinctions and social distinctions create social consciousness. My mother understood that our family could not compete with the affluence of the rich.

"Don't you go to the neighbors so much," she said, "those people are rich. Stay away. We are not rich like them people." Unknown to me, those rich people were about to change my life. I would soon learn about social distinctions through my famous dance performances.

One day, after we tired of playing, my neighbor invited me to his house. "Let's tell my mother to give us a peanut butter and cracker sandwich," he said. I could not refuse. That single statement hooked me and I followed him into their kitchen, a room that sparkled with new chattels unaffordable by the common family.

Discomfort seized me amid all those shiny new appliances. I heard the echo of my mother's admonition, *Those people are rich. Stay away.* I was quite out of place. Guilt clutched my chest. But the desire to have a peanut butter and cracker sandwich soon drove away the omens that prophesied doom.

"Give us a peanut butter and cracker sandwich," my friend said to his mother.

"No," she said, "It will soon be time for supper." She wore glasses that gave her face a near scowl, something I mistook for sternness. Ordinarily, I took such conditions as an invitation to leave, but my friend's next move immobilized me and prevented any escape.

Somewhere in time, his ancestors must have been psychologists. He knew how to manipulate his mother. I determined to learn his skills because I could profit from them.

"I said give us a peanut butter and cracker sandwich." To punctuate his demand he threw a magnificent tantrum. He jumped about, stamped the floor, and screamed. He beat the table with his fists, kicked the wall, and yelled his dissent.

My eyes widened, my mouth flew open, and my mind told me to leave. I was confused, embarrassed, and speechless, not that I would have spoken up though; the prospect of a peanut butter and cracker sandwich was beyond mere words.

All the old demons of insecurity and doubt returned; certainly, I came to the wrong place at the wrong time. Why did I ever enter the lair of the rich? This behavior was foreign to me and unsettling. My parents never allowed such actions. Perhaps I should have listened to those omens clutching at my chest. But all my fears vanished when his mother relented and said she would give us a sandwich.

The admiration I held for my friend now turned to awe. Without question, he was a top-notch negotiator. He was the king of magicians and knew how to make peanut butter and cracker sandwiches appear, like pulling a rabbit from a hat.

She took that cracker container from the cabinet, and the sight of it took my breath. That cardboard box, printed with large blue and white letters, was a design worthy of a Pulitzer Prize. To me, it was a priceless sculpture, and it held, stacked one on top of the other, countless crackers made up of four luscious squares. This would be no cheap single cracker sandwich. An upscale feast awaited us. I, at that moment, realized the significance of *rich*. Rich meant I could have what I wanted when I wanted it.

As we ate the sandwiches, he dined casually and nonchalantly as if having them was an everyday occurrence. I, on the other hand, consumed mine with relish; it was such a treat. I let him know I thought he was the best.

*   *   *

With every step homeward, I planned how I would take my rightful place among the rich. I would use the simple means of persuasion I learned that day. With my strategies fully developed, I strode into my mother's kitchen, a new man, a general on a life-changing mission.

"Give me a peanut butter and cracker sandwich," I demanded.

"Now you know we don't have anything like that; go on and get out of here," she said.

Hearing that answer, I knew it was time to escalate the negotiations. I threw the mother of all tantrums. I jumped about, stamped the floor, and screamed. I beat the table with my fists, kicked the wall, and yelled my dissent. I knew success was near because I used the same techniques that worked for my rich friend.

Some negotiators have more success than others. My mother was a superb negotiator. She knew how to counter-escalate; she knew how to get the opposition to concede a point.

Robert Burns said, "The best laid schemes o' mice and men go oft astray." Looking back on it, I realize he was a prophet. He certainly foresaw my future.

My mother snatched the switch from atop the bread warmer faster than a cobra. She gripped the switch with her right hand and me with her left. That switch lit me up like a light bulb. My schemes went astray and unraveled fast.

"I'll skin you alive, young man. We'll see how well you can throw a fit. Now dance, now dance, now dance!" she said, as blow after blow fell on my back. There was no let-up from the instruction of the switch. I danced the most intricate steps. I was light on my feet as the fast-paced tune of "Ida Red" accompanied me from the battery radio. I did a combination of Irish jigs, fast polkas, and fandangos. At that moment, I invented the disco. Fred Astaire, Ginger Rogers, and Arthur Murray achieved dance fame, but none had my know-how. I can understand their lack of expertise. I had the advantage of expert instruction.

Sylvia Rosenthal

Bits And Pieces

O F COURSE, YOU KNOW I'M GETTING YOUNGER each year. Aren't we all? However, last year was the breakdown year. A tooth literally broke while I was biting a piece of very cold chocolate. Serves me right, you say? I had no business sneaking into the chocolate cache. I keep it way back on the bottom shelf of the refrigerator just to avoid such skullduggery. However, occasionally—maybe a little more often than that—temptation gets the best of me.

Dear dentist told me that the broken tooth was dead, kaput, and had to be removed. After that, there were two choices. He could drill into the two adjacent teeth, file them down into fangs, cap them and create a bridge replacing the broken tooth. Alternatively, he could put an implant into the jawbone and, eventually, if the implant "took" (that is if it attached itself firmly enough to my jawbone so that it would hold a tooth), he could attach a false tooth to the implant without compromising the adjacent teeth. I opted for the implant. I have too few teeth left in my head to take a chance on compromising any of the remaining ones.

There was a downside to my choice. I have to wait at least four months before we know if the implant "took". Meanwhile I warned my friends that, if I look more somber than usual and don't smile very often, it's because I'm well aware of the black hole of Calcutta in my smile. I also urged them to please save any funny jokes until I can fill in that empty space.

The second thing that happened, that year, was that those nice soft thingamajigs, the part of my hearing aids that fit nicely in my ears, disintegrated. I can tolerate when some things wear out. My favorite blouse gets too shabby. Nylons run. Elastic stretches and shreds. But when something I have to stick in my ear to help me hear disintegrates, I'm in trouble. I have to be refitted, then it takes a slow acclimatization process while my ears decide to accept the new foreign bodies that I need in order to maintain aural contact with the world. Oh well, nothing for it but to jump in and do it. I had done it twice before and what choice did I have anyway? It was as *nuisancy* as I thought it would be, but it's finally done. My ears have given up complaining and except for an occasional hearing aid hiss, they have accepted the inevitable and all is well in that department.

But these problems were minor compared to the major fixit event of the year: Cataract Surgery. Dear doctor was kind enough to tell me that cataracts were a normal concomitant of aging. That this was purely elective surgery and wasn't it wonderful, said forty year old Dr. Wonderful, that in this area we have really been able to reverse the aging process and in cases like mine probably make me see better than I ever had in my life. Who said anything about aging? I came to this ophthalmological surgeon for repair of a vision problem not for his philosophy.

The first surgery took place in March. My right eye was done. The surgery was simple, well handled, and I felt coddled and taken care of. There was a minor glitch and the nuisance of eye drops for about four weeks. I could handle that. What drove me crazy was the terrible mismatch between the undone eye and the new one. I lived in a Picasso-esque world. Noses were definitely in the wrong place. Steps and curbs were major hazards. The usual sidewalk pitfalls were even more dangerous when seen double. I weathered that time with just a few flops, minor bumps and bruises.

In September, I had the second eye done. The surgery was much like the first and now I could see, really see, without glasses. I could answer the telephone or go to the bathroom in the middle of the night without first groping for my specs. There was a fly in the ointment, however. I had to use reading glasses to read anything. I had been so near sighted that I never had had to do that before. I bought at least six pairs of readers—one and a half for each room in the house—and I never could find a pair when I needed one. In addition, another strange thing, my eyes had to work very hard and they got tired!

I had never known what people meant, when they said their eyes were tired. It had always bothered me.

When I went back for my final checkup, Dr. Wonderful said that I could drive in all fifty states with no glasses, if I chose to, but the reason my eyes got tired was that one eye was now slightly near sighted while the other was now slightly far sighted. This could easily be corrected with glasses if I wished. Oh yes, I sure did wish. I had been wearing glasses since I was six and a half years old and I missed them. It was nice to see this well without them but it would be much nicer to see, with no effort on my part.

I took my prescription to the local optician and had a great time selecting frames. You see, when you are as near sighted as I had been, you could only wear teeny tiny frames. The lenses were so thick and heavy; the nose could tolerate only the smallest of glasses. Now I picked out the biggest owl eyed ones I could find. If I were going to continue to wear glasses, I would really wear glasses with big dark frames that you couldn't ignore.

Now do you think I'll live happily ever after? Not on your life. These new glasses are bifocals. I'm having an awful time. The best advice I get, says, "Stick them on your nose and wear them for a couple of weeks. You'll get used to them." I'm trying folks, I'm trying.

Meanwhile my younger daughter, Lynn, had the best comment yet. She said, "Gee mom, problems with your teeth, your ears and your eyes. Don't worry. Think about it this way. It's all in your head, Mom, all in your head!"

Elaine Starkman

Allies in Astonishment

WITH MY THREE-YEAR-OLD GRANDSON I dance up San Francisco's hills. People smile as Sammy mimics my every motion, then shouts, "Stop dat song, Ga'ma. Sing da 'bout milky on da wall."

"Five bottles or milk on the wall, 5 bottles of milk. If one of them happens to fall..." I sing at the top of my lungs.

"Four milkies on the wall. Wight?"

"Right!" I shout with joy coming from an unknown source. Sammy just turned three. Though his vocabulary is grand, he doesn't say "r's," and of late, he's begun to stutter. Since Mira's in the hospital with a miscarriage, he says, "W-w-what you doing?" and "I-I like dat!" Has he picked the habit in pre-school? We say "pre-school" these days.

In the park that's what young moms and nannies, not *baby-sitters*, say. I make myself available when my daughter seeks me out and disappear when she doesn't.

Although I'm tired, Sammy wants to play. I've become a nanny to three Asian kids whose grandmas live far away. I wish that Mira would let me do more, but she proves herself stronger than I was as a young mom—the way I tried to prove myself with my mother. I must not say *miscarriage*, but "stillborn." Twenty weeks, perfectly formed eyes, nose, eyes, mouth, arms.

Grandpa Norm is supposed to rest at Mira's, but he does the dirty work. This is the first time we've slept in an old San Francisco house built for working-class families, now unbelievably expensive. The 33 miles to our suburb is close enough. We can always drive home. At first, Brent, my genius son-in-law, who knows everything about technology but nothing about the heart, finally agreed to our staying over a few nights.

"Ga'ma, come here!" I rush to Sam's call, the way Mira would have. At the slide, I create magic games. A few kids join us.

Sammy was born when Mira was 37; I had Mira when I was 25. What a difference twelve years make in a woman's life. She'll return to her work as a microbiologist. I stayed home until I finally reenrolled in SF State's writing program.

Last summer at the pool, Sammy pummeled Mira's legs when she wanted to swim laps. I took him into the women's shower trying to explain that Mommy needs some time by herself, but when he kicked a locker, I grew upset. I haven't tried to convince him of anything since then. Mira never forces him to nap in the afternoon, as other kids do. If he does, he's up until midnight. Yet most of the time, he's shy, a parrot repeating what he hears.

"I'm just learning," I told him, while we played with Legos.

"I'm just l-learning," he repeated, enthralled with the word.

Today the doctor removed the unborn boy. Mira asked to see the nearly five-month old fetus whose legs seemed shaped like Norman's deceased mother.

My daughter lies in her hospital gown, her glasses thicker than mine, her eyes bluer than mine. Because of fever she must stay an extra day. I'd scoop her up in my arms—if she'd allowed me, but it's her dad she seeks out. She lies in bed mourning; I mourn my inability to help. I grieve the muffled sounds of the hospital.

"Miscarriage happens every day," my neighbor says. *"She'll get pregnant again."*

In the renovated kitchen Sammy lifts his brush to his easel. He's tired but won't sleep. I call Grandpa who is building a train set. Grandpa is the wet-pants changer today. I turn on the TV. Sammy's parents have strict rules about TV.

As Grandpa disappears to bring in Chinese dinner, an African-American family in a fine house sings along Sesame Street-style as they train their child. *See what fun!* Brent comes up the stairs calling Sammy for a bath.

"No, Daddy! I'm playing!" He shakes his beautiful red hair. Brent looks at me exasperated.

"All right, Lynne, but he must have his bath in half an hour." He says it harshly as if it's my fault that his son won't listen to him.

I try to make myself invisible. At that moment, he goes to the phone and calls his parents on the East Coast.

"No, don't fly out; it won't change anything," I hear him say. I look out the window thinking, *Let them come, Brent,* but he cannot hear me.

The uncommon ceremony is small. The tiny casket that Mira chose is the size of a shoe box wrapped in white velvet. Daughter, son-in-law and Sammy hold hands, as grandparents stand, silent. The rabbi says neither too little or too much. For once everyone is satisfied. Brent holds up Sammy and tries awkwardly to comfort his wife. He does not let us near her. The March day is magnificent; the northern California cemetery is alive with spring flowers. We stand around the tiny grave, shoveling dirt onto the site while workers wait for us to finish in less than half an hour, then head back to Sammy's home. Norman places a bowl of water and towel in front of the door to wash our hands.

Suddenly, Brent takes Mira's hand and they decide to walk. We return to the house.

Sammy stands quietly by the living room window looking for something. I take the hint. "Let's go outside to the little house and read, okay?" He nods his head quietly.

We enter the yard where we place ourselves in the neighbors' old playhouse. I squeeze inside. I've brought his book on dinosaurs.

"Do you want to sit on Grandma's lap?" I ask. Sammy hoists himself up. I inhale his still baby-sweet smell. We read about T-Rex, how he came to be and how he disappeared into the earth. We're allies in astonishment. I look into Sammy's hazel eyes. He studies my face putting his finger on my cheek.

"Like my baby?" he asks.

I'm taken aback. "Not exactly. Well, yes."

"Look!" He points to the next picture, this city kid who has been to the Academy of Science many times. I'm glad he doesn't ask the ultimate question—where his baby is.

"Look at the little dinosaur, the one who only eats vegetables and one that is so dumb he needs two brains to help him think. "One in the head and one in his tush!" Sammy smiles and repeats, "One in his head and one in his tush. What happened to him?"

"He melted into the earth."

"Did the other dinosaurs know?"

"Some did and some didn't."

"Why?"

"I don't know."

"Ga'ma, why?"

"I can't tell you."

After we finish, I make up games I'd never thought of before. I'm a huge Alice in a small wonderland. Just as I retreat to normal size, Mommy and Daddy return. Mira walks around the little house and spots the book. She takes me aside. "Mom, you could have picked something else. Sammy's already asked if we'll put him in a shoe box too," she whispers with irritation.

"Oh, I'm sorry." I laugh feebly, like my mother, ancient and childlike at the same time. No defenses. I must be strong to absorb my daughter's sorrow.

***

The next day we decide it's best to leave. As Sammy throws a kiss and waves good-bye, my foreign travels flash before me. In Istanbul, I saw a Turk of 60 help his 85-year-old father. I thought of what wisdom is. Now as I wave good-bye to Sammy, I know that he and his unborn brother bring me there.

Christine Tomerson

Life in Captivity – The Grief

Akbuzal, Kazakhstan, U.S.S.R. September, 1940.

*In October, 1939, the Germans retreated and the Russians marched into Po-
land. Hitler and Stalin were allies, and agreed that the Russians would occupy
the eastern part of Poland from north to south. I lived in Lwow, southeastern
Poland. Before the war my father was a judge. When the Russians came they
arrested all lawyers, police and army officers. My father was warned and went
into hiding. We saw him only occasionally. On April 13th, 1940, my mother,
my brother Antek, five, and I, nine, were arrested in the middle of the night by
the Soviets, driven to a railway station and put into cattle trucks. The journey
to Russia had begun. After about three weeks we arrived at a remote railway
station and were driven by trucks to a village where we found out that we were
in Akdendek ,Kazakhstan. A week later we travelled in carts driven by oxen to
a village named Akbuzal. We were told that we had to remain there perma-
nently and were not allowed to go further than one kilometer outside the vil-
lage. We lived with other families in a large long building made out of mud
and straw.*

SEPTEMBER, THE BEGINNING OF THE FALL SEASON, brought
relief from the unbearable heat of summer days and the
swarms of mosquitoes.

My mother was getting heavier in spite of the lack of proper
nutrition.

In our shack we had sheets and blankets hanging from the
ceiling, reaching to the level of the bunks, forming partitions
between each family, giving us a feeling of privacy.

One day Ivan, the *kolkhoz* (communal farm) supervisor, came
and ordered my mother and *Pani*[5] Rzewuska to lift the heavy

---

[5] Pani means in Polish Mrs. or Miss, any woman young or old, followed by either her
first or last name. The usual polite way of addressing.

tables that stood in the middle of the dwelling. They needed one table for their office. Nobody else was around to do it because everybody else was working in the fields.

That evening my mother said that she was not feeling well. She whispered something to *Pani* Irena, whose bunk was at the very end of our shack. *Pani* Irena said to me, "Take your nightgown. You and Antek will sleep tonight next to my daughters."

I found this a strange request but it did not occur to me to question it. I was used to listening obediently to adults out of respect for them. They always had a reason but nobody bothered to explain anything to children.

My brother and I fell asleep immediately. In the middle of the night I woke up to somebody moaning and crying. I listened attentively. I recognized my mother's voice.

As I was about to jump out of bed *Pani* Rzewuska appeared and whispered, "Do not go anywhere near your mother; she is very sick. Pray for her very hard, let's pray together. Our Father who art in Heaven..."

Did I notice tears in her eyes or was it my imagination?

I peeped out from behind the curtain and saw the veterinary doctor sitting on the opposite bunk. I knew who he was because I saw him tending to cows in barns. *What was he doing here?*

Pani Rzewuska said. "Go to sleep now."

But I could not sleep. My body was shaking with fear. I wanted to help my mother and stop her pain. Again I looked out and, as my eyes adjusted to the dim light shed by the only oil lamp placed on the table, I noticed *Pani* Rzewuska and *Pani* Irena, moving silently, carrying towels and a bucket of water.

Eventually I fell asleep. I had a dream that a baby was crying. *Was it a dream?*

When I woke up, the early morning light poured into the shack through the only window illuminating rows of hanging blankets. My first thought was to see my mother. I jumped out of the bunk and ran towards our space.

My mother was still in bed looking very pale and tired. She smiled at me, embraced me and held me close. *Why was she so happy to see me?* I did not ask any questions.

A few days later my friend Ashana met me and asked me, "I heard that a baby was born to somebody. Do you know anything about it?

"No, I don't," I replied.

I knew that everybody was hiding something from me. I could see it by their whispers and glances when I walked into the room.

I asked my mother, "I know from Ashana that a baby was born here. Tell me the truth."

My mother took my hand and we walked out into the hills. The weather was getting colder and dark clouds were gathering in the sky. I had a feeling of foreboding.

My mother looked around and pointed to a pile of stones covering a hole at the bottom of one of the hills and said, "You had a baby sister. She was born two months too soon. In Poland she would have been taken to a hospital and put into an incubator. Here she had no chance of survival. Sooner or later she would have died from childhood diseases or malnutrition. *Pani* Rzewuska baptized her and named her Barbara. The old Kazak Kuran and *Pani* Rzewuska put her into a shoe box and buried her here behind those rocks."

I screamed, "Why did you let her die? Why did you not let me see her? I always wanted a sister. How could you do this to me?" I cried and cried. I mourned my sister.

My mother said, "Be happy that I am alive and able to take care of you. I did not want you to be hurt."

When I calmed down I realized that my mother was right. I embraced her and asked, "What about my father? He will be very sad when he hears the news."

My mother replied, "Yes, he will be sad, but he will understand."

My father was hiding from the Soviets but he would often come at night to visit us. The last time we saw him was a few days before our arrest on April 13th, 1940. He would write to us from Poland to Kazakhstan signing himself Mila, our housekeeper, so his existence wouldn't be revealed.

We walked back in silence to our shack. I tried to accept my sister's death but at the same time blamed the Soviets for all our sufferings.

Donna Van Sant

Swiss Army Knives

D AD LEFT A WHOLE LOT OF STUFF BEHIND. Like so many Depression-era kids, homemade or secondhand was good enough, sometimes even better than new store-bought. And if you did buy store-bought, you comparison shopped and got the best quality you could get for your hard earned dollar. But if one screwdriver was good, two were better and a dozen ideal; you know, backups, in case one or two broke. I learned these lessons well; by the time I was eight years old I had to work an entire Saturday to earn twenty five cents to replace a roll of scotch tape after I used the entire roll wrapping "presents."

As he got older and wiser, dad also became what my generation called pragmatic, and what he would've called—someone else—pigheaded. He didn't trust the government, religion, big business, you name it and he didn't believe in it. He trusted only those who expressed distrust of the same institutions he reviled. So when recession hit in the 70s, Dad got ready for the "coming bad years" with all the supplies necessary to manage on his own: stored food, water, shelter, guns for protection and goods for barter. All the supplies we all should have for an earthquake, or other catastrophic event. When the bad years turned out not to be so bad, he sold or donated most of the freeze-dried food and kept the survival gear, because—well, you know—you just never know.

After retiring from the Oakland Fire Department on the first day he was eligible, Dad banged around for a few years, seeing the world, then settled down and built a small house on a beautiful lot in the Sonoma Valley wine country. He again collected all the tools he needed to make this his final home. Until the specter of Y2K began to appear on the horizon. All the signs were coming back. The chatter from the survivalists became dire. And again, the rugged individualists were determined to weather the coming storm. I began to receive clippings or copies of articles in my snail mailbox, proof that come January 1, 2000, I needed to make plans to get out of the city and head for Dad's newest obsession—a large rambling house on tiny Copco Lake, located on the Klamath River in Northern California.

Once again he stockpiled food: 5 gallon tubs of cracked wheat, sugar and beans. Cans of fruit and vegetables, boxes of batteries, a generator and tanks of propane and gasoline topped the extensive inventory list. Copco Lake was home to many retired and part-time residents, some rugged, off-the-grid survivalists, and just as many naysayers. Dad felt at home in this small independent community with its volunteer fire department, ranchers and libertarian attitudes.

About the third week of January, 2000, Dad called, angry and full of rants. "What the hell? Was this just a conspiracy to dupe people like me? Did I buy into all the fears about hard-coded dates turning back to the year 1900? Nothing happened!"

"Dad, what do you want me to say? I told you us baby-boomers weren't going to let the world go dark." I was a bit smug; rarely did I ever tell my father he was wrong. His anger and frustration with a society that couldn't even fail like it was supposed to came stingingly across the phone lines that weren't supposed to be working.

Dad moved back to his home in the wine country and kept the lake house for long lazy summers, slowly disengaging over the next five years, dealing with declining health and a general disinterest in a world he never seemed to master.

The summer after dad died, in 2006, we decided to keep the lake property for our own use. My husband and I cleaned out the house; there was a room full of 5 gallon food buckets to donate, an exercise bike modified to run a small wheat grinder, and sundry items cluttering up the basement and garage. Sorting through a bookcase full of eclectic reading materials, I found a book I'd given to my father for Christmas several years before. Called *The Story of a Lifetime*, this substantial hardcover book had several hundred pages of questions to answer with room to detail a person's beliefs, history and life details. Having forgotten all about the book, I sat down to eagerly read. The first few pages were wonderfully detailed, but interest must've soon waned as the answers to questions became more and more spotty. I cried as I read the beginning, the inscription *"for Donna"*, and then sobbed when I read *"what would you do if you had one week to live?"* and Dad's answer, *"I would fill this book for you."*

The next summer, doing a thorough cleaning of the old maple chairs, washing the covers and vacuuming the cushion crevasses, I sucked up several objects from recesses my hands couldn't reach. Cleaning out the canister, I found miscellaneous quarters, screws and not one, but five small Swiss army knives. Small enough leavings, but this year I laughed and said "Thanks, Dad."

{ 2 }

Poems

Johanna Best

Embers

Wenn ich einmal nichts mehr bin,

dann bin ich erst alles! J.W. Goethe

(Once I'm nothing anymore, only then, I'm all!)

******

While it still glows

beneath the cinders,

I stoke the dormant fire to

rekindle warmth and light,

a last desire to

spread wings and rise

like Phoenix once

out of his ashes rose.

No longer raging,

contained, yet bright,

it casts enchanting hues

into the growing night.

A spark breaks loose,

darts in my direction.

Was it not Icarus who paid

the final price for wanting all?

Drawn near, I gaze upon

the withering embers

whispering their last,

till they turn white –

Ghostly silhouettes fading

into the comforting

embrace of night.

Johanna Best

Visitor

I had a visitor last night,
a long ago lost friend.
He ambled by, all clad in white;
I saw him round the tent.

He marched out of the mist,
a stunning sight, indeed;
as many times before, he
laid his head upon my feet.

His gaze, so warm and loving,
it tugs upon my heart.
We seem to have forgotten
the many years apart.

I held my breath, stayed still,
lest he would rise and leave.
He lingered for a while,
and set my heart at ease.

In memory we roamed
together 'round the ground;
watched families of ducks
arrowing across the pond.

We saw them climb on land,
unwitting cross our path;
took great pains to safeguard
the little entourage.

He finally did rise, and
nudged me, once again,
I knew it isn't wise
to put him on a chain.

A long last look – he ambled off
vanishing into space. And I?
I woke – and found my face
set in a smile.

George S. Buice

Piano Lessons

I sat down to play
But there was no way
To pry from my fingers
A song

My teacher said wait
Let the impulse abate
When you've practiced
They'll all come along

It's hard to stay slow
To patiently hoe
Those eighty-eight
Devilish keys

To weed out the dross
And hasten the loss
Of missed notes and discords
Like these

I'm chasing the day
I really can play
Those scales and
Arpeggios well

But, damn it, I'm certain
When life lowers its curtain
I'll be practicing daily
In Hell

George S. Buice

Spring in Fall

Cocooned in steel
Concrete endless
Under spinning wheels
I cleave a landscape
Numbing in familiarity

Outside my hurtling cab
Even the air seems tired
Gaunt branches pierce a brittle sky
Over November hills burnt to umber
In the coppery light of a waning year

Restless, curious, my eye
Lifts to the heights
Discovers a whiff of green
Shading brown death

Grass has gambled
On a handful of rain
Rising in millions
Fearless
Its new year awaiting
No solstice

The essence of faith
This common miracle
Lifts my spirits
To unexpected joy

Life renewing unbidden
Keeping this ancient Earth
For all who drive blindly
Fixed on the road ahead

Maya Mitra Das

An Echo of Rahma – *A Historical Tale*

I

The waves of melodies
Echoed from the Past
A Tune of Bhairabi that was played
By my great grandmother
Her room was on the second floor
With big windows and a marble floor
Her name was Rahma.
Olive skinned Rahma with big black eyes
Played her clarinet with a regal smile
Looking like a Sculpted figure
Gold bangles dazzling like stars

II

A Tune echoed from Past
A tune—played by
My great grand mother
Born in the late 19th century
She had talent writing Poetry
Married to young man at sixteen
Who was district judge in that town
The west part of Bengal

III

I used to call her Bima
Fondly she called me Naiyna
Bima was a special person
Co-founded an Institute for destitute women
Far from the big city (Kolkata)
Nestled in small town
Bima started their work
And brought rupees for their craft
To help the poor
Trained herself in midwifery
Assisted delivering newborns
Echoes of tunes from the past
Keep on echoing, till this day

IV

In summer we went on morning rides
Often by the river side
The river Ganges was full to the bank
A steamer whistled and chugged along
While the river flows elegantly,
People at the bank praying peacefully
The cool breeze and tranquility
Refreshed us completely
Time to return came too quickly

V

One day I wanted a real story,
With cups of tea's swirling steam
Bima's eyes sparkled
She started the story
Now Sun came out of the clouds
And spilled its color all around
On return Bima held her Clarinet
Sadly

VI

Clothes from British Isles
Took over the market,
Goods of India   banned
With vengeance
Weaver's thumbs   sacrificed
To stay away from business
And save their lives
Bima's eyes searched a distance
She exclaimed *We must not permit*
With agony an event was organized
The women's group would marched to Town square
And burned clothes imported from England

VII

The women of the town gathered
Rahma led the march right in front
Carrying the national flag in her right hand
She shouted, *British quit India Bande Ma taram*
The women shouted, *British quit India soon*

*Bande Ma taram (**Glory to our Mother**)*
They marched to town square in peace
Followed by police and passersby close
At Town Square they stopped
Clothes from Manchester were gathered
They started a fire on the heap of clothes
Flame rose snaky like smoke

VIII

The mounted police charged their batons,
One by one women fell on the ground
Lying in the river of blood, they
Shouted *Please, please leave our town!*
Bima with fractured arm, bleeding forehead
Held her flag up, screaming
"leave our land; leave our land!"
The news spread like wild fire
The movement rolled from one town to another

IX

The wind chimes rhymed gently
The setting sun spilled its color of glory
The evening's darkness spread the veil
While crickets started their serenade
Echoes from past went on and on
While stars twinkled one by one

The echoes of the *Raga* keep on coming
The tune of Bhairabi that was played by
My great-grandmother

Maya Mitra Das

Muse

The Pine trees stand at the end of my deck
Several grouped together.
I love them.
One is close enough for the touch of my hand.

The trees stand tall, to touch the sky.
On autumn mornings, dew hangs like pearls
Ready to drop.
Misty rays of sun struggle through branches
Framing the Devil Mountain cloaked in green.

Solemn witness to morning ritual,
The Tree stands over me.
In prayer, in search for peace,
I am safely sheltered by its dark brown trunk
And fresh needles of bright green.

A shared breakfast with my bird, Samrat,
Begins a day of busyness.
Samrat's musical speech
Flows to and fro with sighing of wind
Echoed softly by branches of trees.

Off to Children's Hospital—my work place.
Busy list, much to do.
Quick round in-patient short stay.
Transfusion and Chemo infusion.
At last the end of day I slip through stop and go.
At the Tunnel, I breathe easy
With the thought of home and yard,
Welcomed by the joy of my bird and the Tree.

My cockatiel, eager for company after a lonely day.
His noisy greeting summons me to open the cage.
Free at last,
He is on my shoulder planting pecks on my cheek
As the tea kettle sings a beckoning song.

A cup of tea warms my hands, my eyes search for the Tree
My tensions melt away; and I am home.
Duties and list of house work
Fill the quiet evening hours.
Aware my tree offers silent support.

Late now; the birds and squirrels quietly at rest.
The Tree stands tall, looking toward the sky
Awaiting news of the coming night.
I ask for news—will it rain again.
The Tree sways in answer— *Yes it shall.*

Last night's storm had the Tree dancing in the wind.
Whistling through branches about the house,
Playing a Lullaby
On wind chimes singing birds to sleep.
The Tree watched the house and all who are in it.

I will come again in the evening.
Watch the Tree at rising of the moon.
And we shall share the moonlight.
That softly brushes branches of the Tree
Making it dreamy and regal.

The Tree, part of my life
As my muse it has merged and fused with me.
What is this? Pure love!
Is it an abstract entity?
Eternal, primeval, everlasting!
It is the Tree—my muse.
Stately as it is—guardian of my home and soul—
It sends me to a land beyond a land—

Notes for Blue Moon:

In 1947 Professor Joseph Butterworth, an authority on Old English literature was fired from the University of Washington for both refusing to sign a Loyalty Oath and refusing to testify at the House Un-American Activities Committee. After he was fired he sent over 2,000 resumes and did not receive a single reply.

The Blue Moon Tavern was the *avant-garde* hangout in Seattle from the late '40s through the 1960s. It is located near the University of Washington.

Theodore Roethke, Richard Hugo, Carolyn Kizer, Stanley Kunitz, David Wagoner, Tom Robbins, Ken Kesey, Allen Ginsberg, Jack Kerouac and Dylan Thomas made appearances at the Blue Moon. Roethke, Hugo and Kizer were regulars.

Google *"University of Washington History Link"* for more information about the Blue Moon and McCarthyism in the Northwest.

Gretchen Davis

Blue Moon

Fluorescent specter
glows in night
naked
in the arms of the moon

Come hither
hipster's, where wise men sip
and tell tall tales and
loveliest of lies

Where Roethke, Hugo
and Carolyn reigned
Kerouac, Ginsberg,
Dylan, they said
Robbins, Kunitz, Wagoner & Kesey
all pilgrims come
to honor a quiet old man
whose loudest best word
was no!
to the committee

That simple no
gave birth
to this temple of poets
under words
that glow
in the dark

Gretchen Davis

Tangled Hair

(Man)
　　　　　She lies next to me
　　　　Tangled hair on my pillow
　　　　　Sleeping softly now

　　　　Shrill shriek of night hawk wakes us
　　　　　Fiery smile in her eyes

**

(Man-poem to his love)　　Shades keep out the dawn
　　　　Making hands of time stand still
　　　　　You are in my mind

　　　　Always-morning comes too soon
　　　　Faint perfume scent—lingers on

**

(She-answers poem)　　　Such willing bondage
　　　　In thrall of Eros magic

　　　　Sunrise breaks the spell

　　　　Day star moves at snail's pace

　　　My heart longs for moon and stars

~ 88 ~

Carol Emerson

Fall Reunion

If, in the fall,
you should choose to call,
my door will be wide open,
for this would mend my hurting heart
that has been badly broken.

What a joy I would find
to greet you at the door.
Thinking perhaps the time has come...
for weeping no more.

In the daylight a walk in the park,
a glass of wine, after dark,
watching the fire spark.
The smell of pine-fed fire
raising our emotions even higher.

Holding each other,
We'll always remember
staying that way till early morn...
the fire was only an ember.

If you return in the fall rain
we can relive the same refrain.
Although, today, if you decide to stay,
the refrain will not be the same
it will be filled with the hope,
that our love will always remain...

Carol Emerson

Lincoln And Lilacs

...With floods of the yellow gold
the gorgeous, indolent, sinking sun, burning...[6]

Nearby the grey-brown river, churning.
Gathering crowd of towns people
from Lincoln's grave returning.
Passing their Lilac tree, in lavender bloom
take in the essence of heady perfume.
Even with the sinking sun
leaves still shine when day is done.
In the darkness they're still aware
the precious tree is standing there.
Though having lost their President,
and as his soul is rising,
he looks down to inhale and see
the enticing, thriving Lilac tree.

---

[6] Walt Whitman, "Leaves of Grass" 1900

Carol Emerson

Mind Over Matter

What are memoirs?
Stories in time.
What if you wrote them in rhyme?
Would it not be the same?
Writing is creative, not some game.
To create comes from the mind
mine does best in rhyme.
Don't want to waste your time,
it's just my hill to climb.
The rock rolls uphill this way,
but it's how I face the day.
Enjoying words that fit together,
even discussing the weather.
"Hey buddy, it's cloudy today."
"Don't worry the wind will blow them away,
no one cared yesterday."
That's the past, just a memory,
in a memoir, it would be a reverie.
Would you have understood it better had it been prose?
Just remember, "A Rose Is A Rose, Is A Rose."[7]

---

[7] Gertrude Stein, "Sacred Emily", 1931

Roy Kahn

1781

Advice whispered from the grave of the 4th wife of Captain Benjamin Pierce. She predeceased him—as did his other three wives. Their names, dates of death, and causes of death are not mentioned on the "family stone". Stone is dated 1782, the year of the captain-husband's death and bears his name only, and the head-images of his wives. (See 2011 book by Roy Kahn: *New England Gravestone Images 1648-1850*, for image of stone.)

Song Whispered at a 1781 New England wedding.

Women get married,
Amanda, Amanda;
Men get married as well.

The man you must marry,
Amanda, Amanda
Will make your life Hell.

So when you get married,
Amanda, Amanda
When you get married
Remember: Don't Tell;

But wield the axe wisely,
Amanda, Amanda
Wield the axe wisely
and well.

The tree you cut down,
Amanda, Amanda,
The tree that you fell,
If all done a-rightly
Won't be *able* to tell.

Don't cry now, Amanda,
Dear, poor Amanda,
Don't cry on this day as you wed;
There'll be no bell knelling;
You won't have to be dead.
Live *life*, dear Amanda;
No need to live Hell.

Accept God and marry,
Amanda, Amanda,
Since you're forced to be wed;
But, dear Amanda, surely
Remember :
Do God's Will as well.

Roy Kahn

In Rachmaninoff's Green Room,
Carnegie Hall, 1930s

My God, She was beautiful!

> (there, in Rachmaninoff's
> green room, and all the others
> speaking French or Russian)

So beautiful I was Godsmacked.

> (being 11 and just having said
> "bonjour" to Rachmaninoff—
> although it was night.)

If Fate would have it—and she—
I would have lived her worshipper;

> (Her whim, major or minor,
> my absolute repertoire.)

Black velvet dress—a skin to
stir the soul of starbound sailors;
16 years old—an ideal muse
for Dante.

> (but arranged for 11 year old
> playing.)

I was hers forever—if she would
speak to me.

> (brilliant, where she would
> conduct me;)

And I,
mistaking slavery for love,
yearned—scaling the heights
of adoration; hanging there
like an overtone of heaven,

(vaulting and unheard—but
without which no eleven-
year-old's heaven could be
real).

For me, she was more than Rachmaninoff
and all his music
although she made not a sound
—never said a word.

She started it
Nothing could stop it.

Notes fell off the page, clefs came askew!
Like a hapless chord that, flabbergasted,
finds itself transposed,
I silently became another thing
—I knew not what.

She left.
And I was left:
unwritten music,
in a key unknown,
never mastered, never forgotten,
unsung, unrepeatable:

a Rachmaninoff encore

echoes of loves lost,
loves present,
love unmastered;

pain unheard by others—
buried in beauty
present in
Rachmaninoff's green room:
and early love.

Roy Kahn

On Academe:
Possibly the Worst Poem Ever Written

My[8] stomach[9] speaks[10] with forked[11] tongue[12]

Brèthèd[13] long and loud[14].

My stomach,[15] it can do no wrong;[16]

My stomach stands[17][18] above the crowd![19]

---

[8] Immediate self-reference (my head, my heart, my butt). What makes you think that anyone is interested in your "anything"?

[9] Stomach: surely not an appropriate subject for poetry. Reader is probably not interested in your guts.

[10] *Non-sequitur:* Stomachs do not convey information verbally.

[11] The forced accent here, while rhythmically appropriate, is pretentious.

[12] Forkèd Tongue: clever because it makes it seem that the stomach is dictating what its possessor says; but while this may be linguistically associatively correctly located, anatomically and, as an image, it comes close to disgusting.

[13] "Brèthèd": Neologism somehow perhaps related to breathing, which is not even physiologically related to the stomach and suggests ructation; and with two added displaced accents (for rhythmic purposes) adds to the word's already-overweening pretentiousness.

[14] Thus seems to refer to the tongue; creating an image of a long (thin?) tongue (?) doing **something**. Combined with "brèthèd", it leaves the reader struggling for an image of what may be meant or what is going on and what particular ululation is occurring, and from where, and why.

[15] Comma: grammatically acceptable; poetically: nonsense. Also, breaks the rhythm.

[16] "Can do no wrong" is the first phrase familiar to any reader. A relief. But it attributes to the stomach powers over the real world (and those who live in the real world, let alone live there with free will unhampered by stomach-domination). Even with poetic license it is hard to accept an interpersonally active stomach with powers of right and wrong which, assumedly, require if not a brain at least a moral sense.

[17] Now **there's** an image!

[18] Is it floating?

[19] "Above the crowd"—the second commonly understood phrase of the poem, and appropriately occurring at the end of the poem to "pull it together". However, stating or implying that a stomach is all-powerful and superior (vide: "above", above) to all persons, including the possibly deluded poet, is ridiculous and unpoetic despite the advantage it has of being possibly insane.

Jane Louise Loebel

Daddy

Daddy, why did my mommy die?
Why do you come home so late?
I miss you.

Because all day long I work with
your
Grandpapa.

We pick up heavy, dirty pieces
of iron to lug them onto
stretchers.

I am ashamed of this work.
At night I write for a
magazine on children's feet.

Why are you always late?
Why can't I come with you?

My job is to learn the work.
Your job is to go to school
and to learn.

Jane Louise Loebel

Help Want Ad

I want to be loved
by your long
Dancing fingers
Your soft velvet tongue
Your strong gentle touch

I want to be under
Your warm healing palms
Resting firmly on intersections
of spine and pelvis
relieving traffic jams.

Jane Louise Loebel

Vibrations

Autumn leaves
playing among themselves
Colors calling

Reds, burns, garnets
Oranges, mangos, pluots, cabernets
Blood, salt and tears

Born to die
Gray winter sky
Dripping tears

Jennifer MacDonough

Bewilderment

Riding bikes along a path brother and I alone
came across an unknown sight one we'd never seen before

My brother yelled "LION" and we threw our bikes down
we ran as fast as we could into our mother's arms

Out of breath we told her about the lion that we saw
nodding in agreement brother and I

Mother bewildered at what we had to say
and away we went to show her what we'd come upon that day

We turned around the corner and my gosh there it stood
mother held us close to her explaining best she could

Relief and laughter at what we'd seen afar
it wasn't a lion after all—it was a neighbor's Saint Bernard

Jennifer MacDonough

Dusk

Standing on tip toes
amongst whispering trees
gently kissing my husband to be

Strolling hand in hand
by the river's edge
now watching our little ones
dancing ahead

Holding our memories close to our hearts
knowing we vowed never to part

Now in the twilight
a heavenly breeze
having laid you to rest
under whispering trees

David McCauley

Flower Light

One summer solstice
as sun rays fade
and twilight passes,
flowers in my garden
are still awake
with low afterglow

Every blossom shines
with a light of its own,
not as bright as a moonbeam
not as soft as starlight;
like a halo
enchanting, eternal

After a moment of glimmer
they pale,
petals fold shut

As a flame flickers and vanishes
with a puff of smoke

David McCauley

Poem Genesis

Thoughts fly like blackbirds
dropping seeds on ground of memory

All day I stir, waiting for night

Dreamy notions sprout, grow

I wake to graft lines of verse

More nights to nourish
flourish
blossom

More days to prune
sculpt

At last, the poem is born
in my garden of reverie

Email

I awaken sliding arms and legs through sighing sheets
Words come fully formed...
So, hair bristling on legs and head,
I wait for whisperings to gather to obey my strutting will.

Chill chair propping me,
Fingers cocked,

They pounce:

"I woke up this morning to your fragrance in my love-swept sheets."

Take out "up".

"I woke this morning to your fragrance in my love-swept sheets."

Better. Awakened?

No.

Awoke?

No. Don't pick, it's now as perfect as the sky.

"Heading" asks the page, and the heretofore neglected ether shouts perfection at my placement of:

"Haiku!"

"Gesundheit!" is the darling girl's reply.

Rule Rattray

Not So Fast, Honey

"I love you darling," so you said
While lying on your tangled bed,
I felt as if a loaded pistol
Pointed at my pointy head.

Nice thought, but could you grant the favor
Of finding words with truer flavor?
Please, put those words on hold and wait
A least until our second date.

Rule Rattray

The Atheist

I stood with Ed, the atheist
Upon a gentle hill.
The night was ripe for confidence
The air was clear and still.

Ed was looking at the skies
And I was looking too – He said;

"You are my trusted Friend,
Who'll listen to me true.

The stars above look down on us –
Or so the preachers say.
But I look up with wondering eyes
And see another way.

Those tiny lights are blazing suns,
The do not look at us.
Their eyes turn inward toward
The grains of gas and dust
That are their brood, their feckless brood –
They do not look at us.

They say the world was made for us.
Now isn't that sublime?
I say this sun, this world,
This mighty space, this time

Created us.

No need for ghosts.

If you would find a god to love
Just emulate the stars,
And inward turn to look inside
And nurture there the tiny light
That captures kindness and survives.

The preachers' egos shout at us
No don't dare look within,
The God of love's apart from us
To doubt that is a sin.

I've tried my best to shut them out
Ignore their pushing din
And take my chances with this life
Inside this aging skin."

Rule Rattray

The Stripper

(song lyric)

Do you recognize me?
I'm the girl you see
When you're all alone in your room...

Did you ever have a night
When you turned out the light
And couldn't get to sleep
because of my perfume?

I'm the girl you know
that you'll never get
'Cause the man for me
ain't been molded yet.

I'm the girl you've seen
in your X-rated dreams
I'm the girl
That you'll never get.

But you can look.
Yes you can look.
But you'll never get my number
in your little black book.

Neither you my friend, or a thousand more
Are ever-ever-ever-ever gonna score.

Oh. I don't need men,
'Cept to tease now and then.
When you've got that itch
I'm a full blown bitch.

I'm the girl
That you'll never get.

Who Was Dillinger You Say?

Why he's the guy whose knowing grin looked out at us
from dotted page, surrounded thus
with fawning cops who sweat to serve the small town rage
of small town jails for small town wage.

"I'll shake this off," he seemed to say,
"You'll hear from me another day."

He wrote to Henry Ford to say
"Whenever I'm in need of flight
I try to steal a Ford Coupè
to travel swiftly through the night
and thumb my nose at Mr. J.
in bullet spattered getaway."

In tiny banks in tiny towns,
he'd swagger forth and do the deed.
"Just place the money here, my friends.
I'll give it back to those in need."
And if those needy folks were sellin'
rotgut booze and fallen women,
"So much the better!" John would say.
"They need the money just as much
as bloated bankers grubbing such."

A rolling stone who rolled across
the Midwest landscape gathering moss

and burghers reading tabloid sheets
within their secret hearts would weep;
"I've paid my dues, why can't I be
as free upon the land as he?

"If I could only stretch and shuck
these stifling chains
and run amuck across the plains
and sleep in Bide-A-Wee motels
with loose-hipped, lipsticked city belles..."

He's Public Enemy Number One,
declared the soft-necked martinet
and set upon his noble quest
to rid the world of freedom's guest.

And so they found a needy lass,
and bribed her with a freedom pass
and money too, so she could feed
a habit that was much in need.

They bushwhacked him, this cheerful man who
'though he'd shot a cop or two,
had smiled that knowing smile of his
that told the world of outlaw bliss.

Just once to do a deed that sings
and tells the world that moneyed things
don't matter in the scheme of things.

Don't matter in the scheme of things.

Sylvia Rosenthal

Requiem

lean against
plant your feet
press your spine against
the hard gray Catskill rock wall
sharp
jagged
remember
conjure up
recall
the soft feel of me
arms creeping up
breasts
pressing against
moving against
hardening against
the hard feel of you
taut
expectant
leaning against
pressed against
becoming part of
the hard gray Catskill rock wall
spiny
splintery

now tell me it doesn't matter
that was then
this is now

let the soft spray of the waterfall
diamonds cascading
droplets catching color
drip slowly into the center of your palm
rivulets
little pools

remember
conjure up
recall
the soft spray of the waterfall
cool
and sweet
as you kissed the center of my palm
inhaled
drank
that first time
tenderly
lovingly

now tell me you don't care
what was then
is not now

lie down beneath the lilac tree
heavy
with bloom
look up through the purpled green light
smell
the perfume

remember
conjure up
recall

that purpled green light
undressing us
caressing us
dappling us both when first we met
drowning
in each other
beneath the blooming lilac tree

now tell me you are leaving
what was then
that is now

Elaine Starkman

Night Eater

I've eaten chocolates in the bowl,
searched drawers through the night

Kisses, crackers, and caramel bites
I won't dare devour in daylight

What I yearn for I do not know
to end this weakness for once and all

or bleed it slowly
imagine perfection seen

not among butter and cream
but fall back on a stronger self:

When my taste is in need
'tis my soul, not my mouth

I must feed

Elaine Starkman

In Golden Gate Park, Autumn, 2013

Today was the jewel
travelers expect;
for those who live here
we know our climate is erratic.

We walked along studying
historical figures we often ignore.
We lost our way driving here,
coming from the hospital,
not from home.

I wanted to drive for practice
after my accident,
but let my husband drive.
When we sat on a bench,

he took my hand to his cheek.
I teared up, the two of us not
so young and sometimes distant.
Then we walked on

eyeing a young black girl
with a shy smile and asked
if we might give her
                    a dollar.

We gave her two, but when we
saw she had no hands, I wished
we'd given her more, that
we'd talked longer and told

her where she might find work
and, of course, brought her home
to sleep in one of the bedrooms
where our grown children had slept,

but we didn't, my only regret
of the whole day.

Donna Van Sant

The Engineer's Poem

In response to a poetry reading by Indigo Moor

I listened to the gentle man,
engineer by day, poet by night,
as he spun his living dream.
Heard the loving pain, felt
the warm humid night descend
as he melted into his past.

Rich melancholy, served hot
and thick, he flowed like molasses
over streets worn down by a
steady stream of home-town souls.

Going home was coming back,
back and back and back again
a slow circle down
into his former self.

The death, the call,
come home, come back.

I went home with him
carried by his baritone,
the scent of his memories crushing
me, his words a slow dirge,
the funeral of the South.

Whisky and ribs,
pies and greens, Aunties' fans.
Singing and amens, cries and
crying. His pain became mine
until I wished it would never end,
until I begged him stop.

Fiction

Alan J. Gould

Going Home

A WHITE ENVELOPING FLOWER, giant tendrils expanding upward—overpowering. Blinding brightness surrounded him, suddenly, silently. His eyes closed, but the searing imagery remained. Ground trembled and oscillated in waves beneath his sprawled body. His right arm stretched over his head and he could feel strands of hair between his fingers as he clutched the earth. Mud ran warm to his touch. Thunder followed the trembling earth, pounding his senses, crushing into his brain. Suddenly silence and stillness. He opened and rapidly closed his eyes—the brightness remained, open or shut. He lay still, the warm mud oozing through his fingers.

Did he hear sounds, voices, shouts? His ears—stuffed, clogged—sounds indistinguishable, muffled. Semiconsciousness returned with a painful tightness between his eyes.

Can I move? Can I touch between my eyes?

He strained to relax a tensed muscle in his right leg—a throb pierced between his eyes and he lay still.

Don't move. Breathe easy.

The pain eased, and the white flower began to fade in tones of gray from the seared retinas.

A biting chill brought consciousness and shivers that cascaded in pain throughout his torso.

Where are the medics? When will they come? Do they know I'm, here? It's so cold. Where is my rifle? I can't see. Stop shaking, oh god just stop the damn shaking.

He sat by the window and let the telephone poles pass in ordered sequence before his gaze. Shortly after the train left the last station the sun had set and most of the passengers sprawled over their seats sleeping. The weariness of a long trip was tempered by the excitement of finally returning home. He shortened his gaze and saw his reflection in the window and realized how long it had been since he had looked in a mirror, shaving, combing his hair. He touched the forefinger of his right hand to the slab of scar between his eyes. Only a numbness remained. He stroked the finger outward across the right eyebrow until normal sensation returned.

God, what a mess.

The train passed through a crossing, and the horn's wail sang in his ears. His hearing was gradually returning, but he still experienced the rebounding echoes of shrill sounds.

Home soon. I'll be home soon.

Everything would dim in time. A wonder how the body recovers, forsaking dark memories to distant isolations of the mind—all the pain when they found him and cradled his head and legs, easing him onto the stretcher. His breath choked in his throat.

"Easy, soldier. You're okay now. We've got you."

His shirt was unbuttoned at the neck, and the tie was knotted but loose. In the window reflection he could see the rows of ribbons on his chest. There was the story, his life, summarized in bands and patterns of color.

It will be different when I'm out of uniform. I'll walk down the street, like everyone else—no one will know about me anymore than I will know about the people I pass. This is rebirth.

"You're doing great, soldier, really, now try small steps—easy, just one step at a time. Stop, rest—it's okay, you're really doing fine."

"Don't push yourself so hard. Don't worry, it'll all come back to you. It will clear up—trust me—give it time."

Home soon. I'll be home soon. Will the house be the same? It's been so long. The living room, leather sofa under the front window, patterned drapes—were there dishes on the table when I left? Did she smile or cry when she kissed me goodbye?

Pull the burned and torn flesh together—reset the bones— rebuild the broken body—quiet the pain.

Will she recognize me? Does she remember me? Will I recognize her?

He leaned back, rested his head against the seat and shut his eyes. There were his comrades, D Company, First Platoon. They filed by him, smiling, waving—his brothers.

We trained and fought together—brothers. Are they alive? —well? I wonder do they think of me. Did they come back for me? Were they the ones? We'll find each other again, some- where, I know.

I'll take off my uniform. There will be new clothes—shirts fresh and starched in their packing, white underwear. She'll fold the khaki pants and hang them in the bedroom closet. The jack- et with the ribbons will hang in the hall closet, easily accessible for friends to see. We'll walk down the street like all the neigh- bors. Who knew or cared how many of them had beribboned jackets hanging in some closet with gray dust gathering on the shoulders? But this is a good thing and the way such things are supposed to be. Let it all go, get on with life.

He checked his watch. Soon the sun would rise and the train would pull into the station. How fitting, how symbolic, to arrive at dawn. He glanced out the window and things took shape in the grayness. Familiar sights into view. He knew those wooden farmhouses and red barns, the crossroads with the lights flash- ing from crossbars. He buttoned his shirt, tightened and straightened his tie. The sky crimsoned with the first rays of the returning sun. When he disembarked the night chill would be gone and the sky bright.

The train slowed and he grasped the seat arm to steady himself so he could reach for his duffle in the overhead compartment. *Easy does it, now*—no cane—he wouldn't have one. He walked deliberately down the steps one step at a time, leading with his good left leg and bringing the right one next to it before seeking the next step, grasping the bag with one hand and the rail with the other. The sun rose over the terminal roof and sparkled dust in a red glow.

He saw her in the distance glancing around, searching faces. He steadied himself and pulled the duffel strap securely into his shoulder and waited. She saw him and began walking toward him, smiling, arms outstretched, the sun backlighting her hair.

I'm home. I'll put my arms around her, hold her close, feel her warmth next to me before I kiss her. Will there be tears in her eyes? I'll kiss them away. I'm home—find me, take my hand.

His fingers curled in the mud, entangling strands of hair. Blazing flecks of white shards floated down in waves from the burning sky enshrouding him like a blanket of soft snow. The trembling of the earth began to lessen and the body that had throbbed responsively to every tremor lay still.

Stetson Hatbox

L OVE OF FINDING OLD ITEMS IN ANTIQUE STORES that had character drew Deena to a black round hatbox stenciled in gold lettering **Stetson Hat**. The box looked in good condition so she made an offer to the owner of the shop, carried it out and put it the trunk of her car. Odd boxes large or small seem intriguing and mystical. Arriving home the Stetson hatbox joined all the varied hatboxes of different shapes and forms. Deena's collection of multi-colored ballet tights from her earlier rein dancing with a copy Parisian ballet study in San Francisco was tightly packed in a City of Paris hatbox. Belts, scarfs, and gloves were stored in smaller boxes. The maroon velvet box held bracelets and necklaces. Boxes were scattered around her room as dust bunnies scattered under her bed. They all lived there in the same room, including a tarnished engagement ring tucked into a Memory Glass Box.

What to put in the Stetson was unclear when Deena bought the box in San Francisco. As a child she collected old soda bottle caps from vacations spent on the seashore along with brass rings from the merry-go-rounds on the boardwalk. Her most precious keepsake, an old bronze-plated skate key, set in time memories of her childhood. At night, when Deena was ten, her parents turned out the house light for the family's slumber and Deena quietly lit a bed lamp playing and sorting items inside the meringue of boxes.

Examining the box closer she noticed a label printed in red ink with yellow tinges of old paper pasted on the top. The label read:

Lundstroms Men's Haberdashery, Since 1884 Store Number One, San Francisco.

Appearing within the label is a personal name and address:

G. R. Turney
Apartment 504
1740 Broadway Avenue
San Francisco, Ca.

She thought this one had belonged to someone named G.R, someone with a life and history. She'd been on Broadway Avenue in San Francisco many times; the box seemed to fit the décor of her bedroom. Opening the hatbox lid there was a piece of cardboard that sat on the bottom of the box once supporting the brim of a hat. Old tissue paper sat a layer below. Collecting artistic cards over the years from friends and family would be a perfect fit. Pushing the tissue aside as she placed the cards and letters inside, her hand brushed against something at the bottom of the box: an envelope with a hand canceled three cent stamp peeking out from under years of its hiding place. Feelings rose from her body as she discovered the treasure; her heart fluttered and beads of sweat perched on her lips as she dug down reaching for the envelope addressed to:

Gerald Randall Turney
1740 Broadway Avenue
Apartment 504
San Francisco, California

No return address was found in the upper left hand corner of the envelope, just a canceled post-marked 1887.

Turning it over to look inside, Deena felt she was passing a threshold of privacy. As her fingers held the fine linen envelope her head swam with what the next step would be. She passed the unglued flap, reached into the envelope and pulled out delicate onion skinned paper. The letter was written with a fountain pen, the writing delicate with thin and thick lines that curled like feathers on each word. Fragile, neatly folded in nature. The letter began with...

My Dearest Gerald,
Time seems endless when my heart beats with my love for you. The breeze in the trees hold your breath close to my neck as the autumn zephyr wind streams through my soul laced with your shadow. Sweet Gerald, my passage to board the SS William S. Franklin is taking place in three days from tomorrow, my bags are prepared. Soon I'll be by your side and we can start our lives that began last spring in Budapest. My love, I yearn for your touch, to stroke your soft skin on your face, to feel you before me. I know it will be real for me when I see you in nine weeks. Remember the night sky is written for us Gerald; the moon is the beacon of our love. Soon I'll be on the seas that will lead me to you. The swells on the ocean floor will rock me deeper into my heart. Please read the daily ship arrivals when my time gets near. I'll be waving from starboard preparing to run down the plank into your arms.
Love in my heart.
Mattissa Upbright   1887 October 3

Tears streamed down Deena's face, each blink a tear-drop caught in her eyelashes blurring the end of the letter. She sat on the side of the bed and wept for a while. How tender and soft Deena felt inside, to be rewarded with passion of experiencing this couple's love for one another. Cautiously, Deena returned the letter to the envelope, moved the tissue aside, and put back the letter on its original hiding place. Behind the cardboard hat frame she noticed a small newspaper clipping announcing ship arrivals and dock numbers posted for December 1887 Pacific Coast Arrivals and Departures for San Francisco. Listed in the third column was the name *SS William Franklin* in bold print: **Lost at Sea**. Deena began to shake and quiver bringing her almost to the floor of her bedroom. Nausea over took her body; her head began swell with a dizzy haze. "*No*, No, this can't be,"

Deena thought. How did Gerald, who lived on Broadway Avenue, cope with this devastating news? Mattissa and Gerald belonged together; they fell in love in Budapest, she was coming to join him in America and start their lives together as Mr. and Mrs. Gerald Turney.

She recalled what drew her to the hatbox in the first place— to hold mementos that were important in her life. The letter found at the bottom of the box stuffed under the tissue paper and news clipping did not belong to her, it belonged to someone else.

San Francisco was only 18 miles over the bridge. The moon was out when she crossed it that night. She thought of the verse in the letter that spoke of the moon as a beacon of love, gripping how the last two hours had impacted her.

She wasn't sure what to expect when she pulled up at the address. She followed her heart in attempting to return the letter to the owner, knowing it seemed right, walking up the thirty-two steps to Broadway Avenue in Pacific Heights with the black Stetson hatbox in tow. She rang the bell. A voice came over a speaker and asked, "Yes, may I help you?"

"Yes, you may; I'm looking for a descendant of G. R. Turney. I have a package here for him."

"A package? Are you sure you want Turney?" the male voice said.

"Yes. I'm sure I found an old letter that belongs to his family," she stammered.

There was a long silence, then the voice over the intercom announced, "I'll be right down, hold on."

The door opened up and a man with a reddish soft beard appeared. Deena asked, "Are you related to GR Turney?"

"He was my great-grandfather, but died in 1911 at sea. You say you have something that belonged to him?"

"Yes." Deena picked up the hatbox, stretching her hand as the gentleman reached to take it from her. "I collect old hatboxes. I bought this one 24 hours ago. At the bottom of this box with this address on it I found a letter addressed to your great-grandfather. I believe you should have it. That's why I'm here to give it back to its rightful owner."

She passed the Stetson hatbox placing it in the hands of the Turney family, the purest act she could do to honor the love between Gerald and Mattissa.

"Well thank you, what do I owe for all the trouble you went through to locate me?" said the man.

"Nothing, please accept this. I better go now; I'm happy knowing that someone in the family has his possession. That's all I want to do." With a warm smile she started to pivot and began her descent toward the door.

"Wait let me walk you to your car." The man began to follow Deena down the thirty-two steps to the street.

"I don't know what to say. You have given me a gift that is invaluable to me. Growing up I heard many stories of my great-grandfather Gerald."

"What you find in the hatbox may surprise you. When I discovered it, I knew I had to seek out its rightful owner." Deena reached for the door of her car.

"Thank you very much," said Gerald's great-grandson. "I'll go upstairs and look at this new-found part of my family history."

Deena started driving down Broadway Avenue, then glanced in the rear view mirror to see the man wipe a tear from his face, still holding the Stetson hatbox. Continuing down the hill, she too wiped a tear from her face.

Taking in the view of San Francisco, glancing at the San Francisco Bay as ships sailed through the Golden Gate, she replayed in mind what the last couple of hours had been for her. Being a part of a love affair that began half way around the world and that it all started by collecting hatboxes.

David McCauley

Hobos

The call of the open road
Escape from pain of the past
Explore new territory
Follow the river upstream or down
Set up a new campsite
Make new free-spirited friends
Hobos, hungry for good grub and camaraderie, gather together along
the back roads and byways, near America's train yards and bus stations.

ONE AUTUMN ALBUQUERQUE AFTERNOON, Charlie sets up his big pot over the coals and fills it halfway with clear stream water. A line of folks follow the path to the pot and each has a little something to drop in... a bowl of diced carrots, chicken bones with some meat on them, a few hunks of beef, a can of kidney beans, sliced onions, peppercorns, three bay leaves from a nearby tree, more vegetables and spices. Charlie watches and stirs.

An hour later a light breeze wafts a mouthwatering smell across the tramp camp. Mostly bearded men and a few middle-aged women show up at the pot... wearing soiled, smoky clothes... each holding a bowl or tin can. They wander in from all directions as Maggie shouts, "Is it **soup** yet?"

Charlie seizes his massive ladle, plunges it deep into the gurgling cauldron, pulls it out and fills her tin can to the brim. Maggie grabs the old metal spoon from her back pocket of her levis, dips it in the can, and lifts it to her lips. First a sniff and then a taste. Forty eyes stare at hers as she opens them and hollers, "IT'S SOUP!!"

As the line forms by the fire, Charlie tongs out the chicken bones and bay leaves and gives it one last stir. Nods and grunts of thanks charm Charlie as he smiles and doles out the scrumptious soup to the hungry hobos. They gather in groups of three to five and slurp in silence, except for a few "yummms".

Then... voices with stories of the last day or the last years fill the cool evening air as the orange sun drops below the horizon. Now and then an excited voice rises above the murmur. Everyone stops to listen to a tale of joy or woe of being a bum. *"Yeah, I rode that Great Northern boxcar all the way from Wichita to Missoula. It was a great summer in those Rocky Mountains."* A 'specially good story makes tears of delight and sorrow wash over grimy faces. Then it's back to the babble as the firelight takes over.

One by one they stand up slowly, trudge to their campsite, spread out their sleeping bag or cardboard, lay down their weary body, say "Goodnight" to their neighbor, let their mind drift gently through the stories they just heard, and wonder where their own path will lead next. *

* This piece is an example of *flash fiction*, inspired by the movie *Emperor Of The North* with Lee Marvin and Ernest Borgnine, the song *Gentle On My Mind* written by John Hartford and sung by Glenn Campbell, and a memoir by a student in Elaine Starkman's *Writing Your Wisdom* class in April of 2008.

Gentle On My Mind by John Hartford (1st and 4th of 4 stanzas)
It's knowing that your door is always open and your path is free to walk
That makes me tend to leave my sleeping bag rolled up and stashed behind your couch
And it's knowing I'm not shackled by forgotten words and bonds
And the ink stains that have dried upon some line
That keeps you in the backroads by the rivers of my mem'ry
That keeps you ever gentle on my mind

I dip my cup of of soup back from a gurgling, crackling cauldron in some train yard
My beard a roughened coal pile and a dirty hat pulled low across my face
Through cupped hands round a tin can, I pretend to hold you to my breast and find
That you're wavin' from the backroads by the rivers of my mem'ry
Ever smiling, ever gentle on my mind

Marisa Samuels

Nightsong

D URING ALL OF DINNER THE SINGING WENT ON upstairs, and no one said a word.

The dinner honored Dr. Talbot, a veterinarian who had been given a special award for his genetic research at the state agricultural university. He had personally invited me "because you are so committed to your horses." I felt as though I were being honored, too.

I heard the singing as soon as I came in. At first I thought someone had been hired to entertain, but I didn't see anyone. I was reluctant to ask—I'm shy, and was an outsider, after all. Most of the attendees were deans, or members of the board of directors. I had a feeling there were a lot of other major donors there too, judging from the designer clothes and the Hermes bags. Marti, the only other client Dr. Talbot had personally invited, chatted to me about her purse while we ate. "I had to have it," she said. "It's a..." Wisnowski? Wernetski? I didn't quite get the name. Marti didn't comment on the singing.

We were in the "great room", filled with antiques, of a mansion belonging to Nelson Mantle, a well-known Quarter Horse breeder. A widower, I had heard, with one grown daughter, renowned for his stable of halter horses. They don't have to perform, just have perfect conformation and behavior. The handler has the horse stand for the judge's inspection, turns it from side to side, and leads it at a walk and trot in a straight line before lining up for final inspection. I always thought you might as well show Breyer plastic horse models, but then I prefer performance over looks. The singing continued. It seemed to be in another language, because I couldn't understand a word. But the melodies were pleasant enough. Maybe it was sort of a Muzak piped through the house.

Caesar salad, a sherry-laced clear soup, rack of lamb accompanied by roasted potatoes and vegetables—and then chocolate mousse and coffee. I wouldn't need to eat again for at least a day. Finally I was comfortable enough to look around the room, and I saw my home vet, Dr. Marcus. I made my way over to him as coffee time was winding down.

"Hi, Dr. M," I said. The singing had become louder, and I had to speak up.

"Maggie!" He stood up, left his table, and we moved into a quiet corner. "So Dr. Talbot did invite you! He said he was inviting two women who meant a lot to him."

"That sounds like something more than a vet-patient relationship," I said, "and considering my age—and what I think the other woman's age is—I take it as a horse-relationship compliment."

Dr. Marcus winked, and laughed. "Gotcha!"

"Listen, I want to ask you something. I hardly know anyone here and I didn't want to be rude. Why is someone singing?"

"Oh. You don't know about Nelson, then?"

"No. I only know he shows halter horses."

"He used to show cutting horses with his daughter. Apple of his eye, she was, especially after his wife died. The daughter had a terrible fall; severe brain damage. Can't talk, but sings. Sleeps all day, sings all night. Full time caregiver. Most everyone here knows the story, so—"

For the first time I really understood the phrase *it took my breath away*. "How awful," I said.

"He couldn't bear to show cutting horses anymore, so he went to halter horses. He does very well."

I understood. They stood still, moved only when manipulated, like Breyer plastic models. They wouldn't have hurt his daughter.

Elaine Starkman

The Boy With Silver Hair

T HE BOY IS LEFT ALONE to fend for himself in an apartment building full of dry rot, peeling wallpaper, and cracked windows. His mother, a tough woman whose speech is different from those around her, refused to take him along. He knows he is bad but doesn't know why. His father, who never talked, left in a hurry, too. The boy doesn't mind; he's used to staying alone. Sometimes he's like *l'enfant sauvage,* but he's just a quiet boy who roams the hallway, jumps up and down the stairs, slides down the banisters, or goes outside for a peek at the world. It's always too cold, too hot or raining, so he comes back in. Besides, there's always trouble in the streets, people dressed alike, men with huge guns, and he's afraid.

The door of his rented three-room family flat remains open because he feels shut off to lock it. Sometimes other boys come to see him; he knows they come because he has a small black-and-white TV on which they watch cartoons or news with people throwing around other people. To him everything on TV seems unreal, but when the bigger boys laugh, he laughs too. Most of the girls have been whisked away. The remaining boys don't play with him but come up on the fourth floor apartment without supervision. After a while, when it stops being fun, they go home leaving him alone. That's the time he becomes *l'enfant sauvage* his mother warned him about. No one knows what magic the boy does during the nights, neither does he, but when he crawls on the floor eating scraps and scratches himself between his legs, he feels better. His mother shouted that if he didn't behave he'd turn into *l'enfant sauvage*. Sometimes he thinks that is both funny and a good idea; sometimes, he grows afraid.

In the mornings he goes outside to pee because his mother said not to dirty the toilet. Then the enemy might come and say that theirs was a dirty country. Outside, he finds a small dead bush to relieve himself. An old woman from the third floor watches him from her window, and, horrified that he's alone, brings food upstairs to him covered with a real napkin. She's shocked at the flat and hated his parents living there, but could do nothing about it. Besides, she collects the rent for the boss. The boy has no money, so the government lets him alone. The few old men who are around don't talk to the boy, but when another woman tells him he's too young to live alone, why doesn't he come to live with her, he still shakes his head no. Besides, he likes it when older boys come to watch his TV and call him "The Dumb One Who Doesn't Speak," but he knows if he wants, he can speak!

Soon the whole flat is a mess, the once white sheets covering the sofa grow grimy. The kitchen sink is loaded with dishes. The dining room used as a second bedroom is littered with paper airplanes and crumbs. The smelly toilet is stuffed up. No one knows what to do with this boy, including himself. Still another woman, a rare one with a man, thinks of taking him in, but doesn't. Even though the boy forgets his last name, he still knows his first name. The sister of the woman with chunky legs and red house-slippers invites him in. He isn't sure if he should go up to the sixth floor. He's never been up there, but he finally crawls up the long creaking stairway. This woman is also kind to him. He's happy to eat her warm bread, but when she tells him he must wash his face and hands, he jumps up and runs away to become one with whom he loves, *l'enfant sauvage*.

One day the boy disappears. Has he died? Has he finally run away? All vestiges of him are lost. Soon after that, the name of the country disappears from the news, then from the memory of younger people. It is erased from the all schoolbooks.

Somewhere in the world, the boy, now a man, still alive, with silver hair, is the only one who remembers.

ABOUT THE AUTHORS

Deirdre Allan
From keeping journals to writing letters I've always loved to write. It was only after getting compliments from my friends about the news I sent to them from obscure places overseas that I considered taking classes. Elaine Starkman has been my teacher and friend for several years, and thanks to her encouragement I have submitted this piece.

(*Pioneer Baby*, page 3)

Anindita Basu
Anindita Basu (aka Dita) lives in Walnut Creek, CA with her husband and has been living here for the last 38 years. She is originally from India. Anindita writes both in her mother tongue, Bengali as well as in English. She has a collection of short stories written in Bengali, published in 2003. She won the UTSAB award in 2002 in Calcutta, India. Her short story, 'Glass Bangles' in English won the Honorable Mention Award in 2003 (Katha Short Story Contest) and was published in India Currents magazine in 2003. After retiring from her teaching career in 2007, Dita now passionately explores her artistic side in making jewelry. She loves to cook, garden and spend time playing with her grand kids. But most of all—she loves to write.

(*What's in a Name?* page 9)

Johanna Best

Johanna Best emigrated in her youth to settle in the United States. As a child, she lived through the horrors of WWII in her native Germany. The Americans appeared to her as deliverers from the scourge of Nazism. Too busy living and making a living as an R.N. and German instructor, she waited until her retirement to write down the experiences of her life—and her reflections upon them. She now lives in Concord, California.

(*Contrasts—The Right and the Upright*, page 12; *Embers*, page 74; *Visitor*, page 76)

George Buice

Bay Area native
Retired Engineer
I used words to do my work
And now they serve my pleasure

(*August 14, 1945*, page 17; *Max's Rat*, page 21; *Piano Lessons*, page 78; *Spring in Fall*, page 79)

Maya Mitra Das

Dr Maya Mitra Das, MD PhD, studied internal medicine and Pediatrics in India, England and the United States. She came to the U.S in 1973, received her training at Downstate Medical Center and State University Hospital in Brooklyn, New York and completed two fellowships—one for the department of Hematology and Oncology at UCLA Medical Center and the second at University of California San Francisco for Radiation Oncology. She currently serves on the medical staff at Children's Hospital Oakland, California. Her field of work involves sickle cell anemia in children, which she has authored several scientific publication. Her hobbies are poetry, creative writing and performance of Indian classical dance Bharatnatyam.

(*An Echo of Rahma—A Historical Tale*, page 80; *Muse*, page 84)

Gretchen Davis

I am a native of Washington State, growing up in Seattle during the 1950s. Many of the poems and short stories I write are based on the militant unions and radicalism of the Northwest during that period of time. Washington State was once referenced in a comment by the Attorney General as "The Forty-seven states and the Soviet of Washington." My own union experience as a member of the ILWU & Packinghouse Workers Union helped shaped many of my ideas. My father was subpoenaed by HUAC when he helped lead a strike at Boeing after WWII. While doing research for a story I found my name recorded in the HUAC hearings. I was fifteen or sixteen years old at the time. I do not know the reason.

(*Blue Moon*, page 87; *Tangled Hair*, page 88)

Karoline DeMartini
Karoline De Martini put her true loves on hold during a forty year career in teaching, city management and non-profit administration. Liberated by retirement in late 2005, she was "back on the boards" by early 2008, singing, dancing and acting in local community theater and musicals. At about the same time, she found Elaine Starkman's memoir class and hasn't stopped writing since. Karoline says that when she can no longer get up on stage, she'll write full time.

(*Hell in the Literal Sense*, page 23; *Quota Girl*, page 25)

Carol Emerson
I was introduced to Mrs. Starkman in 2006 at Mt. Diablo Adult Ed. That is a story unto itself; we'll not go there now. I learned a lot about writing prose but my favorite thing is rhyme poetry. I have included 3 poems in this book. I hope you enjoy reading them as much as I did writing them. Thank you!

(*Fall Reunion*, page 89; *Lincoln and Lilacs*, page 90; *Mind Over Matter*, page 91)

Alan Gould
Retired attorney. Now a volunteer representing veterans in disputes with the VA.

(*Going Home*, page 121)

Sandy Fitzgerald Higgins
Sandy Fitzgerald Higgins lives in the artistic community of Crockett, CA.

(*Placeholder*, page 28; *Stetson Hatbox*, page 125)

Stan Husted
Stan and Jill Husted were married in Kansas and had two sons. California became home with the first of eight US Navy tours of duty. Continued work in public health brought professional fulfillment. Jill's death from cancer, marriage to Allean, and retirement helped Stan focus on what is important in life. He has started to write about those important things.

(*Romance the Second Time Around*, page 31)

Kymberlie Ingalls

Kymberlie Ingalls has a long history with words. Writing came at a very young age in comedic stories about her celebrity idols. From there she found herself at the age of 14 desperately scribbling out sonnets. Now thinking everything had to have structure, she floundered throughout school trying to squeeze her chaotic life into that box.

It wasn't until she won entry into a workshop at the age of 16 with an award winning poet that Kymberlie found her freedom. Writing became more reason than rhyme, but it wasn't her passion. She was going to be an actor, not a writer! When that ambition, and the notion of stand-up comedy failed, she fell back on her first love of radio broadcasting. The writing continued in anonymity.

With her first blog appearing in 1997, her current network of blogs feature genres of personal essay, memoir, opinion and short fiction. She writes in themes of love, loss, humanity, and her struggles with amnesia, all from her little corner of the world.   writerofthestorm.com

Roy Kahn

On turning 80, Roy Kahn jettisoned his past (and apparently prestigious) titles and activities and became whatever you would find were you to meet him today. At 88, he is: a would-be poet, writer of true tales, and WABDL deadweight lifting World Champion for 2009, 2010, and 2012. His 2010 lifted weight was 210.4 pounds. His best writing is yet to come, and not that heavy.

Jane Louise Loebel

Like these small pieces, an occasional poem appears in memoirs my pen dictates in bed. I am a retired family therapist and loving wife. I am still passionate about learning to evoke sensations in words at age 86.

Jennifer MacDonough
Stepping out of my shadow into the world of writing.

(*Bewilderment*, page 100; *Dusk*, page 101)

David McCauley
Dave McCauley is a retired Civil/Environmental Engineer, formerly employed by the USDA, Forest Service. He began writing his memoirs in 2002 and ekphrastic poetry (poems describing paintings) in 2007. His book *Ekphrasis* has been published by Blurb and Xlibris. His paintings, poems, and fiction describe nature and the human condition.

(*Eagle*, page 47; *Pre-Teen Encounter*, page 49; *Flower Light*, page 102; *Poem Genesis*, page 103; *Hobos*, page 131)

Wayne H. Neal
Wayne Neal is retired and lives in Antioch, California. He was a child during World War II, growing up in rural Missouri. It is from that setting this story was taken.

(*The Dance Lesson*, page 50)

Rule Rattray
I'm Rule Rattray, and I live in a rut in Antioch, CA. It's a nice, comfortable rut, and I intend to stay in it as long as I can. Occasionally, I write poetry, but mostly I write fiction. If you've got a Kindle (or other type of tablet that can use the Kindle format), just type my name into Amazon (search) to find my two E-Books. (I'd be ever so grateful.)

(*Email*, page 104; *Not So Fast, Honey*, page 105; *The Atheist*, page 106; *The Stripper*, page 108; *Who Was Dillinger You Say?* page 110)

Sylvia Rosenthal
SB Rosenthal began writing poetry at when she was about 75 years old. She is still writing. She won the 2010 love poetry contest conducted annually by Benicia Public Library Poets, CA. Her prose and poetry have appeared in local publications in Concord, CA, San Antonio, TX and San Miguel Allende, Mexico.

(*Bits And Pieces*, page 56; *Requiem*, page 112)

Marisa Samuels
Marisa Samuels grew up at Los Angeles stable and taught riding till her 50's, eventually owning her own horses. She rides every day. A UC Berkeley graduate (Sociology); also worked for the Democratic Party. She began writing in Elaine Starkman's classes. She's been married for 59 years, has three children, six grandchildren, and two great-grandchildren.

(*Nightsong*, page 133)

Elaine Starkman
I began to write steadily while teaching in Israel, then finished the M.A. program at S.F. State in 1976. I've always written both prose and poems and taught writing to adults. You can find some of my work online or write *Elaine.starkman@gmail.com.*
My most recent book of poems is *Hearing Beyond Sound.* I'm delighted to teach at Osher Life Long Institute in Concord and grateful to Donna Van Sant for her wisdom and help in ordering our latest work.

(*Allies in Astonishment*, page 60; *Nighteater*, page115; *In Golden Gate Park, Autumn, 2013*, page 116; *The Boy With Silver Hair*, page136)

Christine Tomerson
Christine Tomerson submitted an excerpt from her memoirs. In her story, between the years 1938 to 1969, she describes her life growing up as a prisoner of war on the steppes of Kazakhstan, U.S.S.R., and as a refugee in the mountains and deserts of Persia (Iran) and jungles of Africa. She started writing ten years ago in Elaine Starkman's Adult Education class. Soon her book will be complete and published.

(*Life in Captivity – The Grief (Part III)*, page 65)

Donna Van Sant
After far too many years in the lower rungs of management planning, installing and supporting network telecommunications systems and databases, Donna became a Business Analyst and wrote business and technical documents for those same work groups. Finally, retired and with time to spare, she is finding creative outlet, long dammed, in art and writing. Donna is also taking all her old skills & applying them to her latest "hobby-job" as a Book Shepherd: helping others bring their wonderful, talented writing to the published page.

(*Swiss Army Knives*, page 69; *The Engineer's Poem*, page 118)

www.ingramcontent.com/pod-product-compliance
Lightning Source LLC
Chambersburg PA
CBHW051243170626
46809CB00004B/1470